DEDICATED TO VICTIMS OF THE
2013 BOSTON MARATHON BOMBING

Ever since John J. McDermott crossed the finish line to win the first Boston Marathon on April 19, 1897, over one-half million runners from around the world have flocked to Boston on Patriot's Day to trace his footsteps. Memories of triumph, joy and achievement were shattered on April 15, 2013 when a bomb exploded near the finish line leaving three dead and over two hundred injured. A fourth victim, a young law enforcement officer, was gunned down in the wake of the violence. A portion of the royalties from this book will be donated to The One Fund, established to raise money to help the families most affected by the tragic events that unfolded during the 2013 Boston Marathon.

You can learn more about The One Fund at
https://secure.onefundboston.org/pages/about

Three generations of Brennan runners

TWENTY-FOUR YEARS TO
BOSTON

My Journey from the Vegetable Aisle
to Boylston Street

Jim Brennan

ST. JOHANN PRESS
Haworth, NJ

ST. JOHANN PRESS

Published in the United States of America
by St. Johann Press
P.O. Box 241
Haworth, NJ 07641
www.stjohannpress.com

The paper used in this publication meets the minimum requirements of the
American National Standard for Information Sciences—Permanence of Paper
for Printed Library Materials, ANSI/NISO Z39/48-1992

Interior design and composition by Susan Ramundo
(susan@srdesktopservices.com)

Cover design by G&H SOHO, Inc.
(www.ghsoho.com)

ISBN 978-1-937943-13-4

Manufactured in the United States of America

DEDICATION

To Joanne, for thirty-six years you have encouraged me to be me—
one of life's great wonders; Jimmy, Jason, Danny and Colleen, you inspire me
and brighten my life; Jason and Carley, you never fail to make me smile;
and Gina, Alice and Monty, thank you for coming into my life and
sharing your wonderful selves. Mom, you amaze me; Jeannie, you are brave
beyond words; and Jack, my confidant. Finally, Eddie O'Toole,
you keep me going decades after escape from the vegetable aisle,
and you humor me every step of the way. Never stop!

CONTENTS

ACKNOWLEDGMENTS

This book would not have been possible without the advice and encouragement from each of the members of the Bucks County Writer's Workshop who taught me how to shape my thoughts and ideas into a story. I joined the workshop thinking I was a writer, and you have given me hope that I might be one someday.

CHAPTER ONE

MIRAGE

I pulled a cold Harpoon Indian Pale Ale from a sink full of ice to keep me company in a steaming hot tub of water at the Omni Parker Hotel on Tremont Street in Boston. The hops slid down my throat as I savored that good soreness only a distance runner could appreciate. The paralyzing cramps I'd suffered hours earlier along Commonwealth Avenue were an illusion, and I pondered where I'd run my next marathon. Big Sur along the Pacific Coast Highway was always a dream, and an endurance runner can't escape the hype of conquering the five boroughs of New York City. Hometown Philly would always be an option, but my daughter Colleen was in her final year at University of Scranton, so I could visit her on a mid-November weekend and run the Steamtown Marathon on Sunday.

I pulled another ale from the ice and wondered how I'd arrived in Boston twenty-four years after swearing never to run another marathon. The pain I'd endured during my first 26.2-mile race was so debilitating that it began a two-decade hiatus before my second attempt.

I eased deeper into the water, my head barely above the surface and the cold bottle balanced on a tiny island I made with my belly. I closed my eyes as visions of that first marathon seeped back into consciousness.

. . .

My thighs were engulfed in an incendiary rage as though injected with napalm. I thought my calves would explode and splatter blood all over spectators lining Benjamin Franklin Parkway. There was no way I could endure another step, let alone three more miles. Had it not been for instinct developed plodding one foot in front of the other for twenty-seven years, I would have staggered to the curb, laid down on the cold pavement and surrendered. Instead, I pieced together the final miles of the 1981 Philadelphia Independence Marathon—step-by-step, block-by-block, mile-by-mile.

Oblivious to the stench of garbage that lined Ninth Street in the Italian Market, the thought of suffering through the final city blocks was suddenly eclipsed by a faint murmur of a crowd in the distance. Borderline hallucinatory, my mind plummeted into the depths with my exhausted body; it could just as well have been a mirage. Each step brought closer a distinctive resonance that could only have been cheering. A shot of adrenalin eased the agony and lifted my spirits, which had evaporated somewhere around mile nineteen. The resurgence of energy was incomprehensible, but I didn't resist.

When I rounded the corner onto Chestnut Street and headed toward Independence Hall, what I had thought to be a figment of my imagination came into focus. Thousands of screaming spectators lined the sidewalks and filled bleachers. Though I was depleted of the carbohydrates, potassium and other nutrients that fortify a marathoner's body through 26.2 miles, I was revitalized and sprinted to the finish line.

I limped through a chute that funneled weary bodies to race volunteers who collected bib numbers to record each runner's official time. At the far end of the chute, my family bobbed up and down on their toes, each with an ear-to-ear grin. Nobody seemed to mind hugging my disheveled, repulsive torso, and no sooner did my dad congratulate me than he leaned over, opened a cooler and handed me the coldest, most refreshing beer I had ever tasted.

. . .

Many years passed, and in 2005 it was still a mystery how I sprinted those final city blocks with twenty-six miles behind me. The energy had swelled from deep inside, like an idle geyser that suddenly erupts spraying steam and water hundreds of feet above the earth. There is no shortage of theories that attempt to explain how an athlete pushes through exhaustion and performs during the late stages of an endurance event, but after finishing my first marathon I was convinced the mind plays as much of a role as physical conditioning.

The agony I'd experienced that day was so intense it branded an unwanted, but indelible image into my memory, like a faded tattoo. The purpose of exercise is ostensibly to improve health, and the grueling race left me beat up, run down and bruised—it defeated the purpose. The pain was imbedded so deep into my subconscious that I swore never to run another marathon. But that pact was flawed, for my memory is like that of an elderly man who searches through a cluttered attic to find a misplaced Ted Williams baseball card, when all the time it was in the top drawer of his bureau.

As the years slipped by, I rationalized that distant memory the same way a parent encourages a young child to get back on their bike after a fall, or how an equestrian trainer advises a rider to get back in the saddle shortly after being thrown. Still, I struggled to determine whether the painful memory of the 1981 Philadelphia Independence Marathon was solely responsible for a twenty-year hiatus from competing in another 26.2-mile race.

CHAPTER TWO

THE ACCIDENTAL RUNNER

I began distance running in an era dominated by the Viet Nam War, Woodstock and The Rolling Stones, when runners wore Chuck Taylor sneakers over knee-high sweat socks and drank tap water to hydrate, if they hydrated at all. It was a time when ten thousand meter races, or 10Ks as they are called by runners, were found only at track meets, rather than social events that attracted thousands of athletes who congregated afterward to extol their fitness achievements and wash down bagels with foreign light beer. That someday tens of thousands of runners would register to run 26.2 miles using a medium called the World Wide Web was as absurd as Buck Rogers' tales were to our parents in the 1930s.

I was a nondescript city kid who grew up in a blue-collar neighborhood of row homes in the Mayfair section of Northeast Philadelphia. We played every schoolyard sport ever devised by kids with nothing but time on their hands—stickball, half-ball, wire-ball, wall-ball, touch football, slow-mo, one-on-one, hide the belt, manhunt and jailbreak, to name a few. When I graduated to organized sports, I was an anomaly—I enjoyed practice. A requirement for nailing a spot on the high school football team roster was running a six-minute mile, and I inadvertently discovered an affinity for distance running while training on the hilly trails of Pennypack Park.

During the second session of two-a-day practices at training camp, the coaches would send us into the park for a long run in the muggy Delaware Valley evenings. The other players would be bitching and I'd be near the head of the pack loving the sensation of sweat dripping from every pore in my body. Cleansed physically and mentally, I thrived and couldn't get enough of the heart-thumping, breath-sucking feeling. I referred to the surge near the end of a run as a "kick" long before I'd heard the term used as part of running vernacular. When teammates would suck wind like a bunch of fat, old men, I'd slam the hammer down and sprint to the finish. Though our high school mascot was a crusader, I never suspected those summer runs would begin a decades-long campaign that would lead to a starting line in the small town of Hopkinton, Massachusetts.

In retrospect, my skills were probably cut out for cross-country running, but I chose to ram my head into bodies much larger than my own 5'9" and 150 pound-frame playing football. My teenage rationale was sound—kids on the cross-county team were skinny, wore nerdy outfits, and didn't get drunk on the weekends. But years later my choice left me wondering if I would have enjoyed more success in a sport for which my talents were better-suited. Regardless, those training runs during summer football camp stuck with me after graduation and I found myself on the trail running ten miles just for the hell of it.

Typical running gear during those early years included heavy gray sweat suits and those Chuck Taylors. Running in Chucks was no different than running in your great grandmother's rubber goulashes—they lacked support, barely had an arch and offered little cushion. The science of *air* and *gel* would not be discovered for another couple of decades.

Chucks were little more than a flat piece of rubber glued to canvas intended for playground hoops, but served as all-purpose footwear sharing time as work boots, drinking shoes, dancing shoes and, of course, dating shoes. In the 1970s, it would have been incomprehensible that a movement would evolve thirty years later that advocated running in footwear with less support than present-day running shoes, even barefoot, to prevent injuries and build leg strength.

My insatiable appetite for distance running paralleled the aftermath of Frank Shorter's gold medal at the 1972 Olympic Marathon, a defining achievement credited for introducing the marathon beyond a secluded fraternity to the mainstream. I was oblivious to the rich running history of my hometown, Philadelphia. I'd read in the sports pages that Villanova University had an Ireland connection, recruiting world-class runners like Marcus O'Sullivan, Eamonn Coghlan and Ron Delany. Legendary running coaches Jumbo Elliott at Villanova and Tom Donnelly at Haverford received national recognition for their programs, yet they were merely names I'd seen in the newspaper and heard on the local sports radio. It would be years before I'd appreciate their extraordinary achievements.

During my early running years I was surrounded by fame, and ran in obscurity.

. . .

The sensation of a soaking perspiration flowing down over my body after an hour run felt perfect. I began to run to destinations that were a reasonable distance from home, rather than drive. I would run from home to the gym several times a week, then one day I realized I enjoyed the run more than the workout when I got there. Distance running became part of my fabric, it was my passion.

Friends considered my behavior absurd. That I would wake before dawn or set out after dusk for an hour run was a mystery on the scale of Sasquatch; it left them dumbfounded. They would question my motivation and sanity for running ten miles, and then they'd stare at me and scratch their heads when my explanation failed to satisfy their curiosity.

Somewhere along the line I became an endurance runner, loosely described as an athlete unfulfilled by an hour jog and whose vocabulary contained jargon that include terms like fartlek, carb loading and splits. An endurance runner's idea of a good time is a three-hour run along a hilly trail on a hot, summer weekend morning or a fifteen-mile trek through the forest after work.

I suppose a person who would wake at five a.m. and stretch, scratch their stomach, stretch some more, break wind, then strap rubber to the bottom of their feet to go out into the darkness for a five-mile run is a bit unusual. Equally abnormal is the person who would eat dinner, do homework with the kids, chauffeur them to practice, read the paper, then, just as everyone in the house settled in for the evening, drive to the track to run five miles before going to bed. A reasonable observer would conclude such behavior is eccentric and obsessive-compulsive, embodied by lunatics who need to get a life. Such perception exists because the motives to run are counterintuitive to a non-runner.

Consider that a non-runner rests when he doesn't feel well, sleeps when he's tired, and either gets a load on or takes a day off when he's stressed. A runner's mentality is the complete opposite. A runner believes that running will cure nearly any ailment. After a tiring day, a runner will push through the first few miles of a run and typically feel refreshed. More than thirty years of hitting the trails revealed that running is an effective natural remedy for fatigue, and doctors, psychologists and researchers all agree that running is among the best natural stress relievers.

Best of all, running is self-initiated and requires only a decent pair of running shoes. Running requires no teammates, opponents, equipment or membership fees. It is pure and natural, an activity that closely followed walking after we let go of the coffee table as toddlers. But running does require taking the first step, and that first step is always the boldest, regardless of the venture. It is no different than taking the first step to earn a degree, play an instrument or speak a foreign language. In each case, the reward is worth the effort.

．．．

Throughout my life I'd battled self-doubt, a condition I attributed to being whacked in the back of the head too many times by the Sisters of Perpetual Condemnation during my formative years. The nuns of my childhood wore habits down to their ankles, enough perfume to gag a hooker and were more adept at humiliation than compassion, a formula that instilled fear in my timid little soul. The morning bell in the school-yard would send shockwaves through my body and panic through my impressionable mind.

My earliest recollection of elementary school was an assignment to write a book report that would later be presented to my second-grade classmates. I loved the library, though I lacked the aptitude to read fluidly. Most afternoons I could be found in the library scouring through as many books as I could get my hands on, and I would always check-out the maximum, though only portions of a few of them would actually get read. For the assignment, I'd selected Dr. Seuss' *Cat in the Hat*, a story I loved and couldn't wait to share with the class. When my name was called I walked to the front of the room with anticipation, eager to tell the story of a mischievous cat to my classmates, who would surely enjoy the adventure as much as I did. I no sooner announced, "The name of the book I read was *The Cat in the Hat*," when the nun said, "James, why did you pick such a childish book?"

I froze with embarrassment, unable to speak. I mumbled a few inaudible words, cowered back down the aisle to my seat and buried my head on my desk in shame. The incident launched my pedestrian academic career.

My nickname in elementary school became Dumb-Dumb. The name didn't strike me as unusual considering some of my buddies'—Box Head, Loose Lou, Crazy Mac and Gig—nevertheless, I worked diligently to live up to my reputation. I was a resident of the "Vegetable Aisle," a label my fourth-grade nun gave to a row of underachieving students who, in her infallible determination, were in a vegetative state. We were ostracized, and she would often warn the remainder of the class to disregard us. She mistakenly thought that relegating our wretched souls to the Vegetable Aisle was punishment and humiliation, but I was happy to be a vegetable because she never collected our homework or marked our tests.

This perceived ineptitude was confirmed when I was placed in the bottom of my high school freshman class. There were sixteen classes ranked according to academic performance. Freshman One was full of geeks who wore big glasses and pocket protectors, so I was relieved to be placed in Freshman Sixteen because I'd be damned before I'd be surrounded by those freaks. The proud owner of an inconspicuous academic record, I clawed my way up the academic ladder my sophomore through senior year and miraculously graduated, an achievement I attributed to divine intervention. My sole claim to fame was athletics, and the one thing I could do well was run.

A few years after I graduated high school my buddy Tommy, the first competitive runner and cyclist I'd known before the two sports became popular in the United States, urged me to sign up for my first organized race—a 10K. Tommy came into my crosshairs as I rounded the bend into the final stretch at Liberty Bell Race Track in Bucks County, Pennsylvania. With plenty of gas remaining in the tank, I ran past him as if he were out for a Sunday afternoon stroll. Following the race he talked me into training for the Philadelphia Independence Marathon. I figured that mustering the determination and discipline to run twenty-six miles would prove that nothing was beyond my grasp, and therefore help counter my inadequacies. I rationalized that personal achievement would result in fulfillment and I would find contentment. Shortly after I completed the marathon my euphoria diminished precipitously with time and, to my dismay, left me the same insecure person I was before I'd begun training.

Not long after running that first marathon I embarked on other quests to evict my demons. Convinced that education held the key to shoring up my self-esteem, I went back to school to earn an associate's degree. However, after getting my diploma the insecurities reemerged. I continued my education and graduated Cum Laude with a bachelor's degree in Business Administration in the same inadequate state. I believed career advancement would give me a sense of accomplishment to quell my incompetence, to no avail. No matter what I achieved, I remained restless, looking for the elusive meaning of life. The cost associated with raising a family with four children didn't allow the expendable income to travel and confer with the Dalai Lama, so I was left to my own devices.

Many years of searching left me emotionally unfulfilled. Between diplomas and promotions, I thought I'd covered all the bases and began looking within for a solution to the nagging restlessness at the core of my being. I wondered if the answer I struggled to find lay somewhere within the introspect, persistence, and the blood, sweat and tears that came only from gutting out a race so grueling the mere thought of it is unimaginable to most human beings. Instinct hinted that perhaps I missed something twenty years earlier, during my age of innocence, and I should revisit the challenge of the marathon. The answer to my unsettledness, I concluded, must lie within the marathoner's axiom—beyond the, "Twenty miles of hope," and in the, "Six miles of truth."

CHAPTER THREE

EPIPHANY

On a November evening in 2000, while on business trip, I had an epiphany. It came as I walked down Saint Asaph Street in Old Town Alexandria, Virginia. The ghost of the Philadelphia Independence Marathon had tormented me since 1981, and I was intrigued by the notion of running a second marathon on the twentieth anniversary of my first. The more I thought about the idea, the more captivating it became. If I ran my first marathon at twenty-seven and was forty-seven when I ran my second, would I be tempted to run a third in my sixty-seventh year? I pondered the possibilities.

The enthusiasm permeated every aspect of my life. I couldn't shake the idea no matter how hard I tried. It followed me to work, the pub, even the bathroom in the middle of the night—no, especially the bathroom in the middle of the night. After all, that's where guys do their best thinking. So much had occurred during the hiatus. I had coached Little League, sat on the board of the local athletic association, taught an evening third-grade religion class, went back to night school and earned a degree, switched careers, lost my father, doubled my children, and buried a rabbit, two dogs, six fish and countless frogs.

This time around I'd compete as a seemingly responsible father of two college students, a carpenter and a high school senior, as opposed to an unruly, twenty-seven-year-old foreman welder at the Philadelphia Navy Yard. Back in those days, "Yardbirds," our adopted nickname, would allege that welders were the dumbest of all the trades. I'd convincingly debate that boilermakers and riggers had the corner on the dumbest-trade department, closely followed by a half-dozen other professions. The disputes never come to a decisive resolution, but were always entertaining and good for laughs.

As a foreman responsible for supervising welders in the reconstruction of aircraft carriers, I was in peak physical condition by default. The demands of the job required climbing hundreds of vertical feet each day: ladders seven levels down from the hanger deck to the tanks below, and thirteen decks up to the top of the mast. Many jobsites were in confined spaces that could be navigated only by climbing through tanks three feet high separated by bulkheads with eighteen-inch diameter holes. The sole technique to inspect these jobs was to walk hundreds of feet in a squatting position, which strengthened my legs and glutes like no program a personal trainer in the 1980s was sadistic enough to devise.

Working aboard aircraft carriers also provided unprecedented endurance conditioning in extreme heat because some exotic metals require preheating prior to welding to prevent cracks and defects. Four-inch thick, two and one-quarter percent chrome steel drums were wrapped with insulated blankets and preheated to four-hundred degrees before a welder climbed through an eighteen-inch manhole to weld. The concentration required to lay an X-ray-quality weld while contending with intense heat is unimaginable, but I never realized the job was preparation for a different type of endurance feat. After all, how difficult could running a marathon in ninety-degree heat be after routinely working under such conditions?

To top it off, I rode a ten-speed bike from my home in Cheltenham Village to the South Philadelphia shipyard several days each week, a forty-mile round trip. A typical day would start with a twenty-mile bike ride before a shift began, and then I would climb hundreds of feet onboard ship, crawl through tanks, solve problems and put up with a bunch of shit from construction workers, some of them ex-cons, all the while under oppressive working conditions. When the whistle blew at the end of the shift, I'd hop back on my bike and peddle twenty miles home through some of the most notorious neighborhoods in the City of Brotherly Love with names like the Badlands and Brewerytown. Junkies staggered along the sidewalks and cars whizzed by so close to my skull the heat radiating from their engines singed the hairs on my cheek. I'd arrive home, hop off the bike, kiss my honey and the kids, and take a five-mile run to relieve the stress. Maybe "unruly" wasn't an accurate description—I was probably borderline mad.

Epiphany

I never considered a run at the end of a shift on a smoky, asbestos-laden ship an option, but rather a responsibility. It was the best way I knew to purge my lungs of smoke and hideous asbestos fibers after an eight, twelve, sometimes even a sixteen-hour shift. I knew too many guys who had suffered some form of asbestosis and considered myself fortunate to be able to get out and exert myself athletically. I ran with a purpose for those who weren't so lucky and suffered a slow death from the fibers that infiltrated their lungs. The insidious disease was known to lie dormant for years, even decades, between exposure and when symptoms would manifest, and running was the remedy to flush out my lungs every chance I got. I would run pissed-off that corporations who manufactured the material knew about its health hazards years before occupational health researchers. The men and women who handled the material for a living were never informed about the risks or educated about proper handling precautions. Consequently, in the early days wearing protective gear wasn't an option to reduce the potential of contracting the disease. If that wasn't bad enough, workers exposed their families to the fibers when they returned home after a hard day's work and the kids would jump all over them while they hugged their wives, unknowingly transferring the fibers along with their affection. So in those days I ran for my shipbuilding brothers and sisters.

. . .

The man who emerged to train for his second marathon was a sharp contrast to the one from twenty years earlier. My two oldest boys, Jimmy and Jay, were away at college, my son Dan was an apprentice carpenter and my youngest, Colleen, was finishing high school. My hectic life was complicated by frequent business travel around the country, which made a routine training program virtually impossible. The thread that held my chaotic life together was an angel named Joanne who maintained stability in a six-person household, and juggled busy schedules for four active kids.

I never aspired to be a lady's man and surely didn't deserve the perfect mate, one as beautiful as she was adept at transforming chaos to calm. I never went to pubs to carouse for women when I was growing up; rather,

I went for the shuffleboard, foosball, the rough-touch football league and the pint. Years earlier, I had passively known my future bride from a vast network of friends. Her stunning blue eyes struck me one night when she walked through the door of a Margate, New Jersey club, a moment I'll always remember. *It was those eyes, always those eyes.* And it was always Jo encouraging me to be me, no matter what cockamamie plan I devised—and I had my share of them.

Through it all, running kept me healthy, grounded and sane. Running was the constant that kept the rat race from tilting too far out of balance. Regardless of how out of control things became, the long run on the weekend, usually with my lifelong buddy Eddie O'Toole, normalized my life and brought me back down to earth. O'Toole was my running partner, accomplice, confidant, and therapist—and running was my refuge.

CHAPTER FOUR

THE ESTABLISHMENT

Few authors capture the essence of a runner's mind the way Dr. George Sheehan did in his book *Running and Being* where he contends, "A runner runs because he has to." It is a compulsion similar to that which drives mountain climbers to climb, a skydivers to dive, or writers to write. Health benefits, mental clarity and love of the outdoors are runners most common responses to the question "Why?" but those answers aren't enough to explain rising early in the morning to run before beginning a workday or late at night before they retire. To a runner, such behavior is a way of life.

A runner's lifestyle is reinforced each time a thoroughly soaking sweat flows from their body and endorphins cascade through their central nervous system. Runners strive for these moments, the magical sensation that systematically seals a commitment that extends beyond the immediate activity to infiltrate every aspect of their wellbeing. The lifestyle transcends running to nutritional inclinations, intellectual pursuits, hobbies, sleeping habits and just about every other aspect of a runner's life. Dr. Sheehan maintained that, "Running is the runner's work of art." How true, Doctor! How true.

Running becomes a cycle of continuity, characterized by sharpened senses and a heightened appreciation for all life has to offer. Inhibitions are shed along with the perspiration, and a pureness that is hard to match under any other conditions emerges. The pinnacle of consciousness arrives with sweat streaming from the pores and clairvoyance of mind. It may sound more a religious conviction than exercise, and I find little difference; running is mind, body, spirit.

Commitment and persistence are the investment required to reap the sport's intrinsic benefits. It is comparable to a casual musician who plays an instrument at his leisure but never becomes an accomplished artist. Then, after years of practice, the musician commits to his craft and becomes one with the instrument, just as a runner becomes one with the process of running. It is a magical moment. There is no standard threshold of time when the revelation occurs to a musician, just as there is no finite number of miles or hours on the trail when it comes to the runner. And, it is unlikely that a casual musician will ever master an instrument, just as the casual runner may never enter the euphoric state referred to as the *zone,* that sweet spot of a run when the feet feel as though they no longer are touching the ground. It manifests differently in each individual. But there is no mistaking when the echelon is reached— and once there, a runner never wants to leave.

There came a time when people within my social circle began to define me as a runner. Conversations with family, friends, peers and associates became more of a fitness inquiry sparked by genuine interest about how far I'd run on a particular day or what races were coming up. It was a conversation in which I was eager to impart the lessons I'd learned from my *craft.* My message was unencumbered by conventional running philosophy and popular trends. Rather than a sermon laden with confusing terms like VO2 Max, periodized tables and anaerobic thresholds, my inquisitors would get the straight scoop about the simplicity of running. Perhaps it is because I have a simple mind; it's the way I think. Mothers tell their children to walk, not run, but inevitably most children run by the time they reach the age of three. In other words, running is a primal instinct everyone has performed since as far back as they can remember. It's not complicated.

. . .

I had always marveled how a small cadre of enthusiasts would attempt to impose their influence on large organizations, whether in business, government or the local Little League. As I entered more and more races over the years, I discovered a similar phenomenon in the running community. Though only a small fraternity of the broader running population, this group came to promote the primal activity of running as a sport so complex it intimidated many beginners and outsiders. I would read books and magazine articles that described the process of running as if it were an instruction manual on how to split an atom. It was maddening. I'd get furious and scream, *Stop it already; it's only running!*

As time went on, I came to view this small community as the running establishment, a group trusted as much as I did the IRS. I found no reason to compromise my practices and conform to the metamorphosis of the stereotypical runner they created. I hesitated to join a fraternity that hijacked a sport that survived thousands of years and held it ransom to a rigid list of rules and regulations.

My perception of the stereotypical runner evolved to be a lean individual decked out in a two-hundred-dollar synthetic moisture-wicking outfit, who constantly checked his stopwatch during a run and popped open a ceremonial light beer at the end of a race. He owned the latest running accessories, subscribed to the accepted publications and had the weekend planned around a running schedule too inflexible to allow time for leisure activities. Members of this fraternity obediently conformed to ridiculous rules such as the headset-ban at marathons, which prohibited runners from listening to music through a headset during a race, supposedly for safety reasons, yet promoted the Rock 'n' Roll Marathon series which features rock bands at each mile along the side of the course blasting head-throbbing music—go figure.

The marketing of races, apparel and other products nudged individualism out into the fringes of the sport. I would watch inexperienced runners line up in a large crowd of tens of thousands at a mass-marketed race garbed in high-tech running gear, bottle belts, monitors and water bladders, many who would be gasping after the first mile and sucking down gels and energy drinks as if they were miracle potion that would somehow, miraculously propel them to the finish line for a personal record. I couldn't imagine what was in store for them at mile twenty-three, or thirteen for that matter. Fees were added: registration fees, late registration fees, fees for not driving one hundred miles to pick up their bib and chip the day before the race, and then driving home and back again the following day to actually run the race. I felt sympathy for young runners who didn't know the running scene wasn't always this way, just like young airline passengers would never know what a delight it was to fly before 9-11 when TSA didn't exist and nobody wanted to touch your privates before boarding a plane.

I rationalized this behavior as simply an organizational dynamic when I realized that no community of common interest was free of such factions. There are wine snobs who look down upon patrons who order a house merlot at the bar, cycle snobs who sneer when they pass a commuter on a bike that is not manufactured from advanced composites, and intellectual snobs who get an erection whenever they get a chance to flaunt their Ivy League graduation rings in public—so why should running be any different?

I had encountered self-professed elitists along the trail my entire life who practiced running snobbery by preoccupying themselves checking their monitors or adjusting their gear rather than exchange a friendly nod, as common folk tend to do. I interpreted their gestures as an inference that they considered runners like me to be a lesser pedigree—Neanderthals.

It seemed to me the sport would be better-served if the elite embraced average and beginner runners, just as professional athletes mingle with their fans. British writer Hugh Kingsmill once wrote, "Snobbishness is the desire for what divides men and the inability to value what unites them." Spoken and unspoken gestures of acceptance would leave a lasting impression and attract even casual observers to the sport, but initially I found such nurturing behavior lacking in some members of the establishment.

The sport evolved from when I began in the early 1970's, but I remained grounded in the rudimentary traditions of running. I grew up a blue-collar runner, drove to races in a beat-up Jeep with peeling paint and wore whatever was on sale at the sporting goods store. The only appendage attached to my torso was a headset and I would enjoy a Guinness and a cigar when I crossed the finish line. In my own mind, I wouldn't qualify to join the running establishment by virtue of my bad habits. I figured if I couldn't savor a few vices after an exhausting race, I should consider joining a monastery.

During my most prolific running years, my daughter Colleen affectionately called me "Fatty," because I was rarely caught without something to eat within arm's reach. As I aged, my tendencies switched from ESPN to Food Network and I ranked pepper jack, garlic and the coffee bean as the three wonders of the world. I would pour sugar in the raw into my espresso without giving my triglycerides or cholesterol a second thought, and would return dirty looks with a smile whenever I would pop a full-bodied brew after a race, feeling sorry for the tortured souls who would never enjoy the satisfaction of a hearty stout to wash down a bagel. I shared a sentiment with Doc, the marine biologist from Steinbeck's *Cannery Row:* "The first one is for thirst and the second one for taste."

I wondered how great runners survived the centuries without the aid of modern technologies. How did legendary John Kelley finish fifty-eight Boston Marathons without the aid of a heart monitor, Under Armor, PowerBars, Cliff Shots and Gatorade? The immortal Kelley won Boston in 1935 and 1945, finished in second place seven times, and placed in the top ten eighteen times, all preceding the PowerGel station at mile seventeen. Inconceivable? Hardly, considering his 1945 winning time was 2:30:40, compared to the 2011 winning time of 2:03:02. Technology does have its advantages; however, I was so blinded by the snobbery of a few that it would take years before I developed an appreciation for the remarkable achievements of elite runners and the gear that shaved valuable seconds off their cheetah-like pace.

My nonconformist nature may have been grounds to be categorized as anti-runner, but nothing was further from the truth. I had the heart and soul of an endurance runner; I was merely disinterested in endless babble about every conceivable aspect of running minutia. I tuned-out when subjected to ramblings about personal records or the latest study conclusions on hydration or effects of Glucosamine Chondroitin. Consequently, my misperceptions left me feeling estranged from the establishment. Years would pass before my presumptions were shot full of holes by encounters I had with humble former Olympians, a renowned college track coach and international world-class runners with similar behavioral patterns as my own.

Though I'd never sought membership into their fraternity, I was confident of my qualifications. I'd clocked ten-milers in under 1:20:00, half marathons at 1:45:00 and finished my first marathon in 3:34:39, performance not considered elite by any means, but not too shabby either. So when the self-professed elitist would pass on the trails studiously peering at their time pieces to calculate another split I would just smile. I'd become immune to the indifference of snobs who'd glance in another direction to avoid eye contact. In my view, anyone who competed in a 5K or a half-marathon was a runner, and anyone who conquered a 26.2-mile race earned the right to be called a marathoner.

I became comfortable as a member of a different group of runners who ran for sheer enjoyment, unfettered by fads, trends and silly regulations. My running brethren could be found in any county park, local track or mountain trail garbed in an array of athletic shoes and clothing. They made up the overwhelming majority of runners who trained and entered distance races across the country and around the world. The proliferation of races that routinely swelled to more than 10,000 runners was possible only because the majority of entrants were recreational runners and weekend warriors, not because there were 10,000 elitists. The establishment might have gained control of the media and the marketing, but recreational runners were the economic engine that financed the multi-billion dollar running industry. Without them, the number of businesses that produced apparel, energy drinks, books, magazines and nutritional foods would dwindle and race entries would plummet. Without recreational runners, a flourishing running industry would stagnate. I was proud to be a member of their club.

CHAPTER FIVE

THE LURE OF THE MARATHON

Most people associate the marathon with either the Summer Olympics or news reports about thousands of seemingly eccentric athletes testing the limits of physical endurance. But the origin of the marathon dates back to a Greek battle in 490 B.C. According to legend, a Greek soldier named Pheidippides ran from the town of Marathon to Athens to report that the Persians had been defeated in the Battle of Marathon, and then died shortly after he made the announcement. There are other variations of the story, nevertheless it is widely accepted that Greece is the birthplace of the marathon.

The historical event was commemorated at the 2004 Summer Olympics, held in Athens, Greece, where marathoners ran the same 26 mile, 385-yard route that Pheidippides ran 2,494 years earlier. Little did the messenger know that his name would be associated with organized races of 26.2 miles more than 2,000 years later. Whether he would think it was worth sacrificing his life will never be known.

In the time since Pheidippides' first marathon, relatively small fields of athletes competed in the event. The number of entrants in major marathons didn't begin to significantly increase until thirty years ago. The Boston Marathon, considered by most runners as the most prestigious road race in the world, didn't top three-hundred entrants until 1964. At the 100th Boston Marathon in 1996, the Boston Athletic Association made an unpopular decision and turned away 30,000 entrants. Still, 38,708 lined up for the race. No doubt, such a crowd would have dumbfounded John J. McDermott of New York, who on April 19, 1897, emerged from a field of fifteen runners to capture the first B.A.A. Marathon in 2:55:10, and in the process secured his name in sports history.

Boston is not the largest marathon. There were 46,536 finishers in the 2011 New York City Marathon, with tens of thousands more turned away because of their registration cap. Runners who don't meet specific criteria established by the New York City Road Runners are required to enter a lottery. Being among the field of runners along the five-borough course is so prestigious that entry numbers have turned up for sale on eBay for as much as $1,000. According to Marathonguide.com, more than one-half million marathon finishing times were recorded in 2010, almost 37,000 more than finished in 2009. USA Track and Field's estimate of 25,000 marathon finishers in 1976 provides a context to the magnitude in growth and popularity in the sport.

Female runners are responsible for spurring much of the marathon growth. Women accounted for only 10.5% of marathoners in 1980 compared with 41.2% in 2010. The largest age group among females is twenty-five to twenty-nine, which represented almost 19% of the female field. In some of the largest marathons, young women in the twenty to twenty-nine age bracket outnumbered their male counterparts.

There was a time when distance runners were viewed as fitness freaks or eccentrics. When Frank Shorter became the first American in sixty-four years to win an Olympic marathon, there was no way of knowing his victory would launch a distance running boom that celebrities like P. Diddy and Edward Norton would join thirty years later. The sight of a rapper or an actor making the celebrated run through the five boroughs of New York City was enough to entice even barroom athletes to consider buying a pair of running shoes and lacing up.

Celebrities can't conceal the fact that a marathon doesn't come without significant commitment, sacrifice and pain. Consider seven-time Tour de France champion Lance Armstrong, who ran the New York Marathon in 2007 after his first retirement from professional cycling. When he crossed the finish line he exclaimed it was, "The hardest physical thing I have ever done." At the post-race press conference he continued, "I didn't train sufficiently enough for this. In twenty years of endurance sports, triathlons, cycling, even the worst day on the Tour, nothing was as hard as that, and nothing left me feeling the way I do now." Not that cycling 2,200 miles through the Alps over the course of twenty-three days is a cakewalk, but it puts the marathon in perspective.

The world watched a field of 112 elite runners line up in the sweltering Athens heat to run the 2004 Olympic marathon in conditions that were oppressive at best. Spectators wondered if the athletes could survive physical punishment so intense it could lead to serious injury, illness, or even death. The race proved to be too much for one of the greatest women marathoners of all time, Paula Radcliffe, who walked to the side of the road at mile twenty-three in anguish. A more tragic outcome occurred in 2007 during the Olympic trials in New York City when veteran American marathoner Ryan Shay collapsed at the five-and-a-half-mile mark and died at the age of twenty-eight. It's no wonder that news reports of more than 40,000 amateurs competing in the New York City Marathon and similarly-sized fields in other marathons around the globe leave sports fans scratching their heads.

. . .

Casual observers believe that people who willingly subject their bodies to a punishing 26.2-mile run are out of their minds, but distance runners and endurance athletes view the marathon as the quintessential challenge. The lure of the marathon possesses magnetism as strong as the gravitational pull to a runner, and it becomes a fixation.

A typical scenario begins when someone steps onto the bathroom scale one morning and is disheartened to find they'd gained a few unwanted pounds, and decides to go for a jog. Before breakfast she drives to a local track and jogs a quarter-mile lap, then walks for fifteen minutes. Two days later the jog increases to two laps, followed by a fifteen-minute walk. By the end of the month, she is able to jog one-mile before walking. Six weeks pass and the distance increases to a one and one-half mile jog, and before she knows it she's running three miles at a comfortable pace. The novice runner discovers newfound discipline with her diet along with increased energy, and begins looking forward to going to the track.

One day she is out shopping for a new pair of running shoes, and a brochure for a 5K piques her interest. Figuring she'd already conquered three miles, another tenth of a mile seems a cinch. After completing her first organized race she's psyched and begins conversing with more experienced runners and reads about 10Ks and 15Ks on websites and blogs. Next thing she knows she's teetering on the edge of a 10-miler, which is within grasp of a half-marathon. Before the year is out, the half-marathon is in the books and running becomes an obsession she can't shake. Confident that 13.1 miles is achievable without debilitating pain, she broadens her horizons when she learns marathon season, September through December, is approaching. Running websites and magazines are loaded with advice about marathon training programs, from beginner to elite, and she can't hold herself back.

Inexperienced runners are sometimes tricked into thinking two halves equal a whole, but there's a catch. The marathon cannot be calculated using simple arithmetic, because in running terms, 13.1 miles multiplied by two doesn't equal 26.2 miles. Training for a marathon isn't the same as completing two 13.1-mile runs on two separate occasions. The rule of thumb for marathon training is to build endurance to a twenty-mile or a three-hour training run.

The attraction of the marathon pulls like a riptide and the beginner finds herself looking for a 30K (18.6 miles) race to build confidence. After the 30K and a twenty-mile training run, she is still functional and thinks she has the marathon licked, which is a trap. A first-time marathoner can only learn from experience that the twenty-mile mark is the equivalent to the endurance halfway point of the race. In other words, the final six miles, 385 yards requires as much stamina, perseverance, and significantly more pain, as the first twenty. It is a lesson in humility.

After crossing the finish line, the novice is faced with his hardest decision of her life—whether or not to run another. The answer typically evolves with time. Immediately after the race, the answer is, "No freakin' way." The following day it is, "Not likely." A week later she is scouring websites for her next conquest, and begins training the following month.

With the first marathon logged in the books, the lure remains, but the distance becomes a fascination rather than a rite of passage. The marathon is an endurance runner's paradox—a physically and psychologically punishing test of the spirit and will that they return to again and again.

There comes a point at which the marathon no longer satisfies some endurance athletes' appetite for suffering and they seek tougher challenges, thus the ultra-marathon and triathlon were born. Casual observers might think marathoners are unstable, but consider the ultra-marathon—a race that exceeds 26.2 miles, some more than one hundred miles. The "Ironman" triathlon includes a 2.4-mile swim, 112-mile cycle and a full marathon. Incredibly, registration for some "Ironman" triathlons fill up in only hours and lines often form in the middle of the night for the more popular races, reminiscent of camping out for Rolling Stones tickets back in the 1970s. The incomprehensible Badwater Ultramarathon, a 135-mile California race, has grown from a single competitor in 1977 to ninety-four (eighty-one finishers) in 2011. Badwater competitors endure intense temperatures as they run from Death Valley to an elevation of 8,300 feet up Mount Whitney, past notorious places with names like Coffin Peak, Funeral Mountains, Dead Man Pass, and Hell's Gate. As the great hockey goalie and Philadelphia legend Bernie Parent used to say, "Some fun, eh?"

CHAPTER SIX

TURF

My narrative evolved as I ran the trails of Philadelphia, and germinated into a story on terrain across the country. Countless miles were logged in the city on the River Drives, Wissahickon Trail and Pennypack Park. The River Drive loop is an alluring 8.4-mile course around Kelly Drive and West River Drive, joined by the Falls Bridge and West River Drive Bridge over the Schuylkill River. The Wissahickon Trail is nestled in Fairmount Park, touted as the largest urban park in the world, and offers an eleven-mile loop surrounded by cliffs, towering trees and historical landmarks. Pennypack Park possesses the choice of paved and off-road trails that stretch for an eighteen-mile out and back course.

While countless miles were logged in the city, my home turf was a small community on the western outskirts of northeast Philadelphia called Cheltenham Village, referred to simply as "The Village" by locals. The Village was my home for twenty-seven years and the epicenter of my running territory. The trail adjacent my property followed Tookany Creek and provided the luxury to hop the back fence and "toe the starting line" any time the urge struck. At the end of the short mile-and-a-quarter trail was a cinder track at Elkins Park Middle School, perfect to stretch a short workout into a ten-mile run. Over the years I concocted more courses to break the monotony and extend the distance to places named Ogontz Field, which also had a quarter-mile track, and High School Park across the road with moderate-sized hills that were ideal training terrain.

Business travel expanded the running trails beyond the Philadelphia region. While on the road I ran every chance I got and unintentionally discovered some of the most beautiful trails in the country. I ran beaches on the East and West Coasts, and trails in the Rocky Mountains, the high desert in the Mojave, the great Northwest, heart of the South and countless cities across the Midwest including Green Bay, Davenport, St. Louis and Chicago. All climates, altitudes and conditions were covered. Regardless where I landed—I ran, and as a result I trained on frigid plains, the oxygen deprived Rockies and in oppressive desert heat.

Much of the business travel was to the Washington, D.C. area where two scenic running trails are located—one historic and one rustic. There is no more of an exhilarating nighttime run than the National Mall, the only mall I would willingly visit. Unlike a shopping mall that would require dodging pedestrians standing in line at Auntie Anne's Pretzels or hurrying into Bath & Body Works to buy a fragranced soap, the wide crushed-stone path that dissects the District, from Capitol Hill to the Lincoln Memorial is runner-friendly. The trail is beautiful any time of day, and especially captivating under the lights illuminating many of the nation's most cherished testaments to our heritage. It's hard to rival a run that passes the Washington Monument, Lincoln and Jefferson Memorials, the White House, Smithsonian Institute, the World War II and Viet Nam Veteran's Memorials, or the Wall as it is known to veterans and many from the war's generation, and countless other treasures.

The Mount Vernon Trail, south of Old Town Alexandria and adjacent to the Potomac River, is shared between cyclists, runners and walkers. The tranquil stretch was my escape from the bureaucratic ghetto of politicians, lobbyists and consultants where I would run through rustic woods, past mansions and tastefully designed southern homes to regain my sanity. Across the river in Maryland lies the imposing Fort Washington. The scenery is captivating enough to distract from the labors of a two-hour run, enabling the mind to flow with the rhythm of the Potomac's current, especially in spring when the cherry blossoms are blooming.

Many times the Mount Vernon run would be followed by a hearty Irish meal and a pint of Guinness at Murphy's Pub on King Street in Old Town. Washington, D.C. is largely a transient metropolis and the Promised Land for federal workers and consultants competing for billions of tax dollars, so standing shoulder to shoulder in an Irish pub, listening to tall tales and downing a pint was the perfect remedy to restore the spirit. Murphy's is rich in Irish tradition and warmed by a log fire in the hearth during the winter. There were times I'd stood at the bar, closed my eyes and imagined I was in any of hundreds of traditional Irish pubs across the country.

It is difficult to rank a favorite running trail. Each has a unique personality—Southern California for sunshine and consistently blue skies with the Pacific Ocean to the west and mountains reaching for the sky to the east; the Rocky Mountains for majestic snowcapped peaks any time of year rising above the thunder of raging mountain streams; deserts of the Southwest that possess persistently brutal conditions without apology, but also a unique beauty; and the river trail in Austin, Texas.

The West Coast terrain begins innocently in the south and matures as it ventures north. Sweat dripping from the body in the midst of a long run along the beaches of San Diego and Mission Bay, further north at Santa Monica and Malibu, and countless coastal communities between, is a mystical youth potion. The trails of Torrey Pines State Reserve that rise high above the Pacific Ocean offer a preview of the mountainous central California topography from Santa Barbara to San Luis Obispo and Solvang. The spectacular cliffs at Big Sur are enough to entice a runner to enter The Big Sur International Marathon, and then the road eases into Pacific Grove and Monterey before reaching San Francisco. A tour along the Pacific Coast Highway has such a wide array of environments, it is possible to feel as though you had run in several countries in a matter of days.

Summit County in the Rocky Mountains has a maze of bike paths and off-road trails, and where there are none you blaze your own. The communities of Breckenridge, Frisco, Copper Mountain and Vale have a network of well-maintained trails shared by all sorts of outdoor enthusiasts and used by locals for commuting. Adjusting to the altitude is a challenge for those who live near sea level, but the adjustment is worth the experience of running while surrounded by majestic mountain peaks wearing snowcaps year round.

The desert's personality invites exploration on foot. A perception crafted during childhood by cartoons depicting skulls and vultures, heat radiating from the sand and arid landscapes sparsely dotted with cacti belie extraordinary beauty that is difficult to ignore. It's understandable how curiosity could lure a naive Philadelphian visiting Phoenix and Tucson on business past a trailhead to explore the Arizona desert.

Running in the desert requires vigilant hydration, skin protection and care to maintain a sustainable body temperature, but with proper preparation the reward of unique landscapes, beautiful vistas and flora not found in cooler climates are well worth the venture.

My biggest surprise came in Austin, Texas. I expected cowboy territory, but instead found a funky runners' haven. The humidity can make the heat feel more oppressive than the desert, but the energy of Town Lake, which parallels the Colorado River is captivating enough to carry a runner beyond a planned workout distance. The river trail offers options including the Mopac Bridge that leads to Zilker Park and the Barton Creek Greenbelt with choices to run anywhere from six to twenty miles. When I visited Austin the temperature exceeded ninety degrees and the humidity was brutal, but conditioning from years of summers in the Delaware Valley made it tolerable.

The criterion I use for a good running trail begins with environment, but also includes convenience, distance, surface, and terrain. Distance running is a solitary endeavor and at times it can be tempting to quit after a few miles. Alone with only your thoughts, a runner uses different methods to stay engaged and motivated during a long run—streaming music through a headset, meditation, or a mantra—but a scenic environment is a runner's best friend.

Running in so many diverse environments gave me an appreciation for the passion and enthusiasm of runners everywhere. Regardless the domain, a runner's stride produces the same effect at sea level as it does at 10,000 feet, and though sweat may pour a little harder in the desert than in the Pennsylvania countryside, the sensation is unchanged. Distilled to its essence, running is universal.

. . .

The upside to business travel was experiencing many wonderful places and people—the downside was being away from my family. Parents with young children can relate to the competing demands of the job, family, home and extracurricular activities, and understand how a training program can easily get bamboozled when priorities clash. The only solution for dealing with unexpected phone calls to pick up or drop off the kids, community activities, leaking water heater, power outage, unplanned family obligations, sick child, leaking soil pipe, sick dog, stopped up toilet or a buddy who stopping by with a six pack, is to be flexible. These are the same reasons business travel helped my training program, because once a workday was over on the road there was no competition for my time.

I was the anomaly of a business traveler. The number one priority for most people I'd traveled with on business was to find the best happy hour in town; mine was to plan the best location for an hour run. Not that I had an aversion to cold beer, but a vigorous workout enhances the taste of the suds. Most times my associates would leave word at the hotel lobby desk or on my cell phone where to join them, but sometimes they'd wait in the hotel lounge until I returned. When they chose to wait, I would amuse myself by stopping before I showered and watch them cringe as I approached, soaked with perspiration while they stood around the bar in their casual attire. I was also assured plenty of space on the elevator going back to my room, yet another of the many intangible benefits of being a runner.

Dorothy had it right in *The Wizard of Oz*, "There's no place like home." When I wasn't on the road, I spent as much time as I could camping, fishing, playing ball and coaching my kids while they were growing up, figuring you get only one tour through life and it goes pretty damn fast. Now, when I look in the rearview mirror of my life, I am reassured there was no more rewarding experience than raising my children. It is increasingly satisfying to watch them grow into adulthood, make their own decisions and independently succeed in life. It is a gift that never stops giving. Today they are as busy as I was at their age, but we get together often to run, cycle or just throw a party and behave like children ourselves. I believe the trick to staying young is to never lose the child inside, regardless your age.

CHAPTER SEVEN

PHILADELPHIA — 2ND AND 20

The epiphany I had in Old Town Alexandria was no longer an idealist's vision to find solitude and meaning. It had morphed into a daunting challenge, made more intimidating by a twenty-year absence from the marathon circuit. Before long I realized coming up with the idea was the easy part. The tough part, surviving a twenty-six-mile race, required a plan, preparation and months of incredibly grueling work. I'd need to adopt a disciplined training program to push beyond the comparatively casual 10Ks and half-marathons that had kept me content for two decades. I'd learned from experience to avoid sprinting out of the starter's box so I wouldn't burnout early and abandon the goal. Rather, I approached the marathon like a mountain climber prepares to conquer Mt. Everest—in stages.

Training for a marathon is a commitment of time and energy. Most marathon training programs range from twelve to sixteen weeks and include long runs, hill workouts, speed work and intervals, which alternate high and low-intensity levels. An easy workout or day off is scheduled periodically to allow the body to recover. Even though I hadn't run a marathon in twenty years, I selected an intermediate training program because I had a head start as a lifelong runner. I broke the training program into two phases: Phase I would be the informal part of the program and include a circuit of races in the Philadelphia region beginning in December, which would be interim goals to help stay focused and motivated. I calculated I'd have to begin Phase II, the serious portion of the program with strenuous, regimented workouts, by the end of July to be in condition for the November marathon.

For no particular reason, I began to keep a record of my training sessions. I'd never kept a running log or diary, but found myself writing notes after most workouts in pursuit of my second marathon. Before long the notes accumulated and I created a file that chronicled my progress.

The races I choose included a 10K in West Chester, PA, the Penn Relays Distance Classic 20K in April, Broad Street Run ten-miler in May, Distance Run Half-Marathon in September and the Marathon Tune-Up 25K sponsored by the Northeast Road Runners in October. There were a few other races of varying distances I would enter when the urge struck. In addition to the training program, I decided to get somewhat serious about toning down my vices, which was a challenge in itself.

Brian's Run, a 10K I discovered while Jimmy and Jay were attending college, is hosted by West Chester University and became my kick-off for Phase I. The race originated in 1978 as a fund-raising event to benefit a West Chester Henderson High School football player who sustained a life-threatening spinal-cord injury during a scrimmage at the age of fifteen. Brian's friends organized a one-time race hoping to raise $500, but the first year 2,000 runners showed up and raised $20,000. After 1979, Brian felt he had benefited enough from the proceeds and asked that others benefit from the event. Since 1980 the race has raised funds for disabled people from the community and today the proceeds assist physically challenged university students needing assistance to complete their studies and maintain an acceptable quality of life. Over the years, locals have been joined by national and international runners and the race received national recognition from *Runner's World* magazine calling it one of the "100 Great Races".

I was surprised when Colleen asked if it was too late to register, not because it was the day before the race, but that she was interested in running a 10K at all. Colleen ran track in school, but preferred the high jump, hurdles and the relays to long distances. I'd run races with Jim, Jay and Dan, but was thrilled to share my passion with my daughter, who was at the age when most teenage girls wouldn't be caught dead with their father in public.

Colleen inspired me with her toughness. Aside from holding her own with three antagonist brothers, she overcame challenges associated with scoliosis, which required a restrictive body brace twenty-two hours a day at the same time she was adjusting to freshman year in high school. The challenge didn't diminish her drive and motivation to train for gymnastics the two hours free from the brace. As her season progressed, she decided she wanted to coach rather than compete and the gym owner hired her on the spot. That was a valuable life lesson at sixteen—if you don't ask, the answer is always no. Scoliosis kept her from running track her freshman year, but she returned the following year and went on to compete in the Penn Relays as a senior. Now she taught me a lesson—step outside your comfort zone and pursue your dreams. It wouldn't be the last lesson my children would teach me.

The race started at midday, apparently the only way to get college students to run a 10K after partying well into Sunday morning. I was excited to run with my boys, even though it was obvious they were appeasing their old man by running a slower pace when they surged the final mile to show me the difference twenty-five years makes. Still, Colleen and I weren't far behind and finished with a respectable time. It was the longest distance she'd ever run, and when I looked into her eyes I had no doubt the accomplishment she felt.

The December 10K was the last race on the calendar for the year, but I still had to survive the festivities of the holiday season before I bid farewell to 2000. Phase I of the training program kept my metabolism elevated enough to ward off any excess weight from homemade recipes and libations, but having the 2001 Philly Marathon in my sights didn't hurt either.

. . .

Joanne and I walked through the door at one a.m. on New Year's morning, an obvious sign that age was sneaking up on us. However, our reward was the rare treat of an empty house. We celebrated the solitude with a fire in the wood burner and a movie, topped off with a nightcap. It was the first time I'd gone to bed before dawn on New Year's since childhood.

I'd taken off from running in past winters, but began to realize the longer I abstained from exercise as my metabolism slowed with age, the longer it took to regain conditioning. Some experts estimate aerobic conditioning begins to deteriorate after only two weeks, so I decided to join the year-round club, those runners I was always quick to ridicule.

The New Year brought what some runners consider a nemesis, but I looked upon with favor—snow. Though snow presents a challenge to running quality miles outdoors, it is a good excuse to lie around or go tubing. Despite the obstacle, the inherent workout of winter activities kept my cardiovascular system pumping. Shoveling a 150-foot sidewalk and a seventy-five-foot driveway, and splitting wood for the stove were at the top of the list. When I installed the wood burner in 1987, I underestimated the workout from lugging tree stumps onto the chopping block, extending a twelve-pound splitting maul above my head and letting it fly. I would drive through the neighborhood with logs and tree limbs loaded inside my Jeep and strapped to the roof returning from a fuel hunt, indifferent to the curious looks I received. I didn't care because a large haul translated into hours of splitting logs, which was an exhausting cardio workout.

During extended periods of poor running conditions, I supplemented splitting wood with light-weight workouts. Splitting wood and weight training was a combination that rivaled any gym regimen. Physical fitness professionals recommend weight training as you age to maintain muscle tone and prevent atrophy, advice I chose to adopt as I approached the half-century mark. I supplemented morning sessions with core muscle exercises, which most trainers consider mandatory for endurance sports, and began to feel fit in a way I hadn't felt since high school.

After ten consecutive days with the thermometer below freezing, the final days of January were in the fifties. Snow melted, the ground thawed, everyone had a sore throat, and there wasn't a suitable surface for running in the region. Outside the back door, Tookany Creek Park was soft enough to swallow a pair of running shoes and the local track looked like a trough hooked up to an overflow valve on a cesspool. I had to revert to running in the street, shielding my eyes from oncoming headlights in the morning and evening and sucking exhaust. I prayed for better conditions in February, but weather in the Delaware Valley is unpredictable; sometimes you could get a Yankee winter and Southern spring during the same week.

Conditions improved the first weekend in February and I was finally able to run on a dirt trail that wasn't ankle deep in mud. Tookany Creek trail was dry enough to run my first 10K of the year and I began to formulate a strategy for the next few months. I was content to stay in reasonably good shape until the Broad Street Run in May, and then extend the distance beyond ten miles during the summer.

After an extended layoff, runners typically feel lethargic, foggy between the ears and generally listless, but once I was able to squeeze in a few long runs that familiar feeling returned. A soaking perspiration, clear head and energized spirit told me all was well with this old man.

CHAPTER EIGHT

SELF-INFLICTED DISTRACTIONS

Determined to stay in reasonably good running condition, I began to log nearly thirty miles per week—not an unusual workload for a seasoned runner, but a range I normally wouldn't have reached until late spring or early summer. It was unrealistic to expect to be consistently motivated during a training program that spanned many months, so when I began to feel fatigued I listened to my body and scaled back. Joanne sensed my sluggishness and reminded me I wasn't nineteen anymore and convinced me to schedule a checkup.

My father had seemed in relative good health when he died of a massive coronary at sixty-five, which triggered a heavy dose of anxiety and chest pains of my own. Though chest pains had been a concern twenty years earlier, I now ignored them, naively thinking exercise was a panacea, even though I knew of world-class marathoners who had dropped dead at an early age. Joanne persisted, so I scheduled a physical exam and stress test. The cardiologist found that I had a prolapsed mitral valve, a relatively common and non-life-threatening condition. Otherwise, he said the stress test showed that I had vital signs of Olympic proportions and a strong heart. I told the doctor if he didn't tone down the complements, I'd be forced to celebrate with a six pack of Guinness and a cigar.

· · ·

Martial arts had always fascinated me, so out of curiosity, I signed up for an introductory Tae Kwon Do class. During the initial interview, the master told me that running wasn't the healthiest form of exercise for an aging body. I found his observation interesting because up to that point

I never considered that I was the owner of an aging body. He went on to explain about the impact that running inflicted on the knees and how it compressed vertebrae. I thought about how I'd cracked my back for years and how my neck felt jammed after a long run. Nevertheless, running had been part of my life for as long as I could remember and I wasn't about to abandon it for a sport I was merely exploring. The master would have to be more convincing before I would change my ways.

The first lesson I learned from Tae Kwon Do was that stretching was fundamental to martial arts—and not the kind of stretching practiced by runners. This was contorting the body into positions that didn't seem natural. I learned to stretch every muscle in my body—legs, hips, stomach, back, rump, arms, neck and feet—in directions I didn't know they could bend. After a few sessions I began to understand what the instructor meant by nimble—he'd always say, nimble this and nimble that. Whenever we'd practice positions or spar he'd coach from the sidelines, "Be nimble." It eventually sank in. I'd always avoided stretching, but once I began to feel nimble, I became an advocate.

After the final session of the introductory program, I was scheduled for a second interview with the master to tell him my decision as to whether I'd commit to a long-term program. I had tried to integrate two divergent sports, but found it was impossible to remain committed to both at the level each required to do them competently. I was committed to the marathon, and though martial arts complemented many aspects of my running, it was completely different from endurance training. I adopted lessons I'd learned about focus and flexibility, and became a more nimble and agile runner, but Tae Kwon Do didn't give me that sensation I got at the end of a long run with perspiration dripping from every pore in my body and that good healthy exhaustion.

As if Tae Kwon Do classes weren't enough of a distraction, I satisfied an itch I'd been unable to scratch for over twenty years and, in March, put a deposit on a Harley-Davidson. Initially, I thought martial arts and a motorcycle didn't figure into marathon training, but as time progressed the seemingly unrelated interests sharpened my focus on running goals. The Harley deal fell through, but I was back in the market.

· · ·

Self-Inflicted Distractions

The Broad Street Run is an annual Philadelphia tradition with a course that dissects the city from north to south. The course travels nearly the entire length of the main artery that begins at the city's northern border with Montgomery County to the stadium district in South Philly. The finish line changed over the years from JFK Stadium to Roosevelt Park, then to its present home at the former Philadelphia Navy Yard at the foot of Broad Street. The runners are greeted as they enter the industrial complex by screaming fans in front of the old Marine barracks to the left and mothballed naval vessels to the right.

In past years, I turned up the training intensity to run Broad Street in April, but in 2001 I scaled back. The short sabbatical after my bout of sluggishness and the stress test, combined with the diversion of martial arts training and renewed interest in getting back on a two-wheeler led to a refreshed running perspective and restored relative sanity. I didn't obsess about not completing a ten-mile training run before the race, as I had in past years, because I felt stronger and more confident while running in the six to eight-mile range.

Over the years, each of my boys joined me down Broad Street at one time or another. I'd begin training for the race no later than mid-February and planned to build up to an eight mile run before I'd be confident enough to attempt the distance. Amazingly, Jay would simply wake up the morning of the race, stagger from bed, sleep in my Jeep on the ride to the starting line, then get out and run ten strong miles. To rub salt in the wound, or out of sheer boredom, around mile three he would say, "Hey Dad, I think I'm going to pick it up a little," and cross the finish line before I reached the intersection of Broad and Pattison, a mile from the finish. It was another reminder about the effects an additional twenty-five years has on the body.

I ran the 1980 Broad Street Run in a small field of runners that made the final lap around the track in old JFK Stadium where the Wells Fargo Center now stands. In 2001 roughly 4,500 runners participated in the race, compared to a field that was capped at 30,000 in 2010. I never dreamed in those early years that one day my children would join me, let alone that they would finish well ahead of me. But those memories increased my appreciation for having a healthy body and gave me incentive to keep lacing up the running shoes and, "pickin' 'em up and puttin' 'em down."

The Broad Street Run became a custom and marked the beginning of the longer distance races I'd enter throughout the year. I looked forward to the crowd and the characters that would line both sides of the street the entire ten miles. Large crowds could always be counted on at popular spots like Temple University campus, City Hall, Avenue of the Arts, South Philly and the stadium district. I would look for some of the familiar sights, like the drummer who always pounded away at curbside in North Philly; I'd smile at the great memories of Smokin' Joe Frazier as I passed his former gym at Broad and Greenwood Streets; I'd high-five Fast Eddie "The Gov" Rendell, who stood near the Academy of Music at Broad and Locust Streets nearly every year, always with a cup of Dunkin Donuts coffee in one hand and high-fiving runners with the other; and then the track team from my high school alma mater, Father Judge, would be manning the water station at Broad and Pattison Avenues less than one mile from the finish line. There was also the sad memory of the forty-five year-old runner from the Port Richmond neighborhood, husband and father of two daughters, who died of a heart attack right in front of us at Broad and Brown Streets in the shadows of the Divine Lorraine Hotel during the 1998 race. My buddy Tommy's brother, John, a priest, who had joined us for the run that year stopped right there on the warm asphalt and prayed beside the fallen runner. I would bow my head and bless myself at that spot every year thereafter.

Broad Street would be different in 2001. I wouldn't be running with the usual suspects—my boys, Ed, Tommy and his brother and sisters, and stray runners from the neighborhood who needed a ride. Jay came along to shoot photographs and his friend Chad kept me company on the ride down, but he was a college cross-country star and I'd see the back of his head for only the first quarter-mile and then he'd be gone.

Although my training miles were down compared to past years and my focus had been sidetracked, I had regained my strength on that sunny Sunday morning in May. I was psyched when I arrived at the staging area at Central High School Athletic field and decided to line up with the six-minute-mile pace group and hang in with the faster runners for as long as I could. I got off to a strong start, and never let up the entire distance, crossing the finish line at 1:15, my best time since 1993. I was outclassed by Chad, who won his age group coming in just over 55:00.

By my calculations, I figured he was eating his second bagel as I rounded City Hall near mile six. Nevertheless, a 7:30 pace for ten miles boosted my confidence for the journey that would culminate in November.

With Broad Street in the books, I alternated between cycling and running and registered for mid-distance races during the summer to prepare for the Philadelphia Distance Run, which would mark a ten-week countdown to the marathon.

. . .

I had booked a cruise to Bermuda for the week following Broad Street to celebrate our twenty-fifth wedding anniversary. A cruise is the mother of all eating festivals, with literature that boast that the average person gains five pounds while out at sea. I searched countless running sources and wasn't able to find a cruise marathon training program, so I devised one that worked perfectly.

1. Refrain from stepping on a scale.
2. Limit to four meals a day—roughly half the number offered.
3. Skip the sit-down breakfast and stock up on fruit, juice and yogurt at the buffet.
4. Don't start drinking until after a daily workout.
5. Schedule an early daily workout.
6. Dance until the nightclubs close to burn calories from the four meals and alcohol.

I didn't eat and drink myself to death, and I didn't gain a pound, which rendered the cruise training program a success. The cruise ship had a track on an upper deck, but I recalled a colleague who was a former aircraft carrier captain tell me he attributed both of his knee replacements to running on the unforgiving steel surface of an aircraft carrier flight deck, so I refrained. I was never fond of the treadmill; however the soothing list of the vessel and view of the aqua-green oceans and blue sky outside the deck-high windows kept me content. A morning workout was followed by a light, healthy breakfast, which transitioned into a few beers at poolside, before a full itinerary that ended on the dance floor around three a.m.

. . .

When I returned from the cruise I bumped into a neighbor who became an unlikely running partner and training advocate. Built with short, stumpy legs and a low center of gravity, Mack was not your proto-typical runner. He had the strongest trunk I'd ever seen of any guy, as opposed to most male distance runners who were lean and taut like steel cables on a suspension bridge. I'd run behind women in long distance races with Mack's lower body development, and they all seemed to get stronger as the race wore on. I would marvel how a little fireplug of a runner seemed able to run strong, forever. I was looking for motivation to keep focused until the big race, and Mack became that motivation.

I was traveling on business more than I was at home during June, but to places with familiar running trails so I was able to squeeze in quality workouts. I was in Washington, D.C. the second week in June, one of the hottest and most humid weeks on record. Temperatures pushed near one hundred degrees with one hundred percent humidity. The first evening after work, I changed into my running gear, ran south from Dupont Circle on Seventeenth Street, past the White House and proceeded to the National Mall. It was a familiar run that I loved under humane conditions, but borderline unbearable in the roasting temperature. I had to keep reminding myself it would pay off down the road.

The following week, Coronado Island in the San Diego Bay was as pleasant as Washington was unbearable. Every day the temperature was in the mid-seventies with low humidity. My biological alarm clock sounded to East Coast time early Monday morning, so I put on my running gear and headed down the coast toward Imperial Beach. As I broke a sweat my view panned from out into the Pacific Ocean, inland across the San Diego Bay and up into the distant mountains, and I couldn't help thinking about where I'd come from and where I was going. Twenty years earlier I was climbing through tanks on aircraft carriers and crawling into manholes to weld boiler tubes. Now I was running down the west coast on a crystal-clear morning preparing a presentation in my head that I would deliver to over one hundred attendees at a defense industrial base conference. My former coworkers were welders, boilermakers and ex-cons, and now my associates were directors, senior executives and flag officers. It was hard to pinpoint when and how my life had changed so radically, and then I noticed the easy rhythm of my breath in unison with the soft pounding of my heart, and felt the sweat dripping from my face down onto my bear chest, and realized it really hadn't changed at all. I was on a long run, just as I had always been.

A morning workout was a perfect beginning to the West Coast swing, and I had to remind myself I was there on business. The week continued in the same manner with invigorating weather, great scenery and a full schedule of orchestrating a conference. I'd begin each day with an early morning run and conclude the afternoon session with a five-mile run. I ate more than usual and had a few more beers than I should have, but I maintained conditioning.

June was over before I knew it and I woke up July 2nd to a crisp, clear, seventy-degree morning and took a customary run to celebrate my forty-seventh birthday. I snuck out the back door while Colleen was sound asleep upstairs and ran a strong 10K, integrating sprints up the hill on the side of the Elkins Park Middle School track. I'd become increasingly contemplative when my birthday arrived, grateful for my health and the things I was able to do physically. Motivation to maintain good health increased proportionately with age as I neared the mid-century mark. I'd listen to co-workers' conversations about cholesterol levels and colonos-copies and tried to change the subject to the Stanley Cup playoffs or *The Man Show*. The more they'd share their health issues, the more resolute I became to continue doing what I was doing to stay in shape. The harder I worked and the more perspiration that flowed from my body, the more I understood the Eastern philosophy that professes unity of mind, body and spirit.

The wave of low humidity continued into July. I ran my first thirty-mile week and had to restrain myself from getting overzealous. Phase II, the formal training regimen, would begin sixteen weeks prior to the marathon, which I calculated somewhere around the end of the month. Mack planned to begin his own serious training program in mid-July, and I was buying time looking for any excuse to delay the more arduous routine until closer to September, but knew that was unlikely to happen.

• • •

In mid-July I took a test ride on a 1999 Harley-Davidson 883 Custom Sportster. It was the first time in twenty-two years I was on the drivers' seat of a motorcycle and it took about five seconds to recapture the fever. Some family members and friends thought that I was going through a mid-life crisis, but I knew it was much different. I was picking up from where I left off when I decided to sell my Triumph 650 years earlier, a purely economic decision that didn't rank a motorcycle very high on the priority list while supporting a family of six on a welder's salary. That made buying the Harley particularly exciting. It was the first toy I could afford in over two decades, and every time the 883 cc's kicked over was a reminder.

After we concluded the deal, Ted, the former owner, told me to follow him. He hopped on his Dyna and led me along winding roads through the rolling hills and rich farmland of Bucks County, Pennsylvania to a biker bar hidden in the middle of nowhere and treated me to lunch. When we pulled into the parking lot and shut down the engines, he looked at what he described as a "shit-eating grin" on my face, and knew I was hooked. We ordered a couple of burgers and beers and sat outside on the deck soaking up the sun while watching vintage motorcycles pull into the parking lot. I leaned over and said, "You know what, Ted? I don't feel like I'm a biker."

He smiled and said, "Yeah, well guess what," peering over my shoulder at a Shovelhead that pulled into the parking lot. "You are now."

I sat thinking, What the hell is wrong with this picture? A forty-some-year-old aspiring marathoner sitting on the porch of a biker bar devouring a half-pound burger and greasy waffle fries, juice dripping down the side of my face, and washing it all down with a couple pints of lager. After a hearty belch a vision of crossing the finish line appeared—the race was only a few short months away.

The Harley experience taught me that true motorcycle enthusiasts possess the same level of passion for motorcycles as devoted runners do for running. Both get a glimmer in their eye when they are totally immersed in what they love to do. While riding on River Road along the Delaware Canal in Bucks County, I would see a look in the eyes of fellow-bikers similar to that of fellow runners' when pushing through the threshold on a long run. No difference.

. . .

The next morning I woke to a seven-mile run that cleared the cobwebs from my head. The funk I'd been in earlier in the year was an aberration and I realized I'd been so focused on running that I was overlooking other needs. One night in July I was taking out the trash and bumped into Mack as he walked down the street with his daughter. He asked how my training program was progressing. A wave of guilt swept over me because I hadn't started the grueling Phase II of the program—I was still having a good old time enjoying my races and taking leisurely ten-mile runs. I fished out an excuse that he somehow bought.

Though I'd stuck with Phase I of the training program as planned, I knew it was time to transition to serious training. I'd worked hard to get into the best shape I'd been in twenty years, but the grueling work had not yet begun. It was time to bear down and trade my Philly cheesesteak and six-pack habit for carbohydrates, protein, fiber and potassium.

Mack advised me to print out a training schedule and tape it somewhere I would see it regularly. I followed his advice and was happy to find I was ahead of schedule on the intermediate program I selected, already in the mid-thirty mile per week range. Unbeknownst to Mack, he gave me the wakeup call I'd needed.

CHAPTER NINE

AWAKENING

The following entry to my chronicles was dated July 28, 2001:

As the training program progresses, I feel my spiritual needs are taking a backseat to all the other stuff going on in my life. Sometimes I feel guilty because I only pray when I need something. Not material things, but more often it's concern about those close to me, like praying that the kids find happiness and fulfillment in whatever direction they take in their young lives. If my faith were like a mustard seed I would trust my loved ones to my Lord's will and I would have no worries. John the Apostle wrote, "If you will ask anything in my name, I will do it." I should learn from a lifetime of experiences that my prayers are always answered His way. I wish I could learn to just let it go.

Two days later, a crisis occurred that shook my life. Joanne called my office around nine-thirty Monday morning, her voice cracking with emotion. When she finally gained composure, she told me that a biopsy performed on two moles removed from Jimmy's back a week earlier were malignant. He had melanoma. The long, drawn-out pronunciation of each syllable of that dreaded word made me cringe. We were devastated. All of a sudden work, marathons, pints, Harleys—everything was insignificant. I became preoccupied and unable to concentrate on anything. Only Jimmy's health mattered.

There is no way to prepare for the shock of such devastating proportions. It comes from out of nowhere and takes the wind out of you like a punch in the stomach. Before that blow I'd always had the ability to take bad news in stride and play the role of the ultimate optimist. I'd reassure the people affected that things happen for a reason, that nobody is given more than they can handle, and to have faith that all would work out. But when bad news knocked at my door I was challenged to practice what I preached—a humbling lesson.

My first born, the unrelenting prankster, eternal optimist, adventurer; the child I played baseball with until it was so dark I never saw the ball that hit me right between the eyes, the one who introduced me to Beavis and Butthead, Jackass and South Park, had melanoma—cancer disguised with an gentle label.

Jimmy shook off the initial blow much easier than we did. By evening he was dissing Joanne about buying cheap sunscreen when he was a baby, "Probably from the dollar store," he joked. He strummed his guitar impersonating the most annoying musicians imaginable and raised the volume a few decibels when he sensed something grabbed our interest on television. He wasted no time planning to go down the shore the following weekend. If he gave a shit about his diagnosis, he didn't show it. He had the perfect attitude to get him, and us, through the ordeal.

The malignant cysts were removed the beginning of August. He went to work in the morning and left to have surgery, like he was going to have a cavity filled. When I got home that afternoon I was shocked to see a patch on his back the size of a sheet of loose leaf paper covering an incision that looked as though it was made with a meat cleaver. But it didn't stop him from going downtown to South Street with his friends that evening.

I was apprehensive about being away from home on business travel, but followed Jim's example about moving forward with life and left for Washington the next morning. My twenty-year old taught me that delaying plans in the face of adversity, especially things beyond my control, was a waste of time. After years of raising children, the tables continued to turn as they reminded me of lessons I'd somehow lost along the way.

I set out for Springfield, Virginia, at four-thirty a.m., an ungodly hour to be awake for any reason other than to go on a shad fishing excursion. Business travel had been part of my routine for so many years that I'd considered it part of the job; however this time I regretted having to go. Though I was completely confident Joanne had everything under control and I could be home within a few hours in an emergency, I felt physically detached. It was an unwanted feeling that grew with time.

At the end of eight hours of monotonous meetings that were apparently interesting to someone, I planned to hit the trails after I checked in with Joanne, even though a code red heat advisory was in effect. Jo reported good news that Jimmy's chest X-Ray results were negative. Two tests remained—a biopsy and blood test. We all needed to move forward, so I sought the relief of a soaking perspiration on the roads of a rural Washington suburb.

I was in the middle of a short five-mile run on an obscure side road in Springfield, Virginia when my right foot slipped into the loop of my left shoe lace and sent me flying. I did a summersault, head missing the curb by centimeters, and ended up in a seated position as if waiting for the judges to hold up scorecards. A stunned father walked by with three young children staring at me incredulously and asked, "Are you okay?"

I thought for an instant and replied, "Yeah, great." I took a moment to re-tie my lace then got up and continued on my way, passing the astonished father and kids and shouted, "Hey, thanks for asking."

"You're welcome," they responded in disbelief.

The run, fall and rebound all began with the news about Jimmy's test results. The enthusiasm and optimism I'd grown accustomed to throughout my life was returning.

The night I returned from Washington, Joanne and I took a walk through Tookany Park along the same trail we'd strolled with the kids when they were young; the trail I'd run hundreds of times. It was obvious things had taken a toll on her. She was brutally honest and said, "It's been hectic between Jimmy's health and being home alone with the kids while you're traveling all over the place."

Joanne's remark shook me. All the years we'd been together and all we'd been through, I'd never heard her express displeasure about anything. It forced me to look within and I admitted, "Look babe, it's been difficult being away from home recently. I guess Jimmy's ordeal affected me more than I realized. I never worried before, because you're so good at handling things. It always seems that when I go away things are running smoother when I come home than when I left. But I can't help being optimistic about the future and spending more time together as the kids get older and more independent."

The subject turned to the kids' future and we agreed each of them was feeling good about themselves and the direction they were going with their lives. During the time of adversity, our relationship grew stronger.

The following week I returned to Virginia for more meetings. I checked into the Springfield Hilton and called home to let my geographically challenged partner know I arrived safely and to remind her where I was. I'd traveled to the DC area often, and infrequently to our Seattle office, so she'd get confused and wonder if I was three-hour drive away in the nation's Capitol or a six-hour flight away to the farthest northwest state in the country. Just as I had sensed emotion in her voice when she called my office a few weeks earlier, I felt positive vibes before she gave me the news that Jimmy's pathology report was negative, the biopsy was clean, and blood tests were negative as well.

Until that moment I hadn't given much thought about how Jimmy's health had preoccupied my life. I never considered his condition was with me every hour of every day, even in my sleep. When Joanne gave me the news, I instantly felt tension drain from my body that I hadn't realized was there. I was free.

CHAPTER TEN

BREAKTHROUGH

August heated up and, to my angst, business travel persisted. Fortunately, things continued to settle down on the home front and Joanne was in complete control. The point of no return had arrived and I could no longer delay Phase II of the training program. I planned a two-week vacation at the end of the summer into Labor Day weekend when the pace at work usually waned. As it turned out, the office was a madhouse, the busiest it had been in years, so it was perfect timing on my part to escape.

I spent the later part of the week preparing the Harley for its maiden voyage to the Jersey Shore. The small town of Sea Isle City would be the longest venture I'd taken on a motorcycle in over twenty-five years. I checked the oil, tires, shocks and gas and all systems were go. Saturday morning I woke to a glistening sun shining in my face—perfect riding conditions. I helped Joanne and the kids pack the car, the entire time itching to kick over the 883 cc engine and head east. From the moment I crossed the Walt Whitman Bridge over the Delaware River to the time I smelled the salt air crossing the Great Egg Inlet, I reveled in the glory of creation. I navigated the back roads of New Jersey, miles of wilderness full of pine trees and dotted with lakes and an occasional backwoods pub. Guiding the shiny hunk of steel through the wild was so much fun I didn't stop once for a beer. When I arrived in Sea Isle I had a sore face from the ear-to-ear grin I wore the entire two-hour ride. I felt like a teenager again, and resolved to hold onto the feeling until the day I moved on to a better place.

The night before the ride I loaded up on reading material for the beach, my usual pre-vacation ritual. I broke tradition and chose Doctor George Sheehan's *Running and Being* rather than another Steinbeck novel, as I had in summers' past. Doctor Sheehan was the first writer I'd come across whose words resonated, clearly articulating the feelings I'd experienced during a lifetime of running. His words captured the essence of the transformation I'd experience whenever I'd strike a rhythm along the trail. Just as John Lennon was known as the "Thinking Man's Beatle," I considered Doctor Sheehan the "Thinking Man's Runner."

Throughout the years, running had evolved from a way of staying in shape to a lifestyle that pervaded every aspect of my being. It was present when I woke in the morning, it affected the way I ate, influenced my daily activities and was with me when I retired in the evening. Doctor Sheehan wrote, "True, running does not fill my day. But it influences the rest of what I do and how I do it. From it comes my role and the style in which I play it. In it I find myself and my design. I start in play, use myself increasingly, and end in joy."

Some refer to running as an addiction, but I consider it a healthy obsession. Addiction has negative connotations, while running is a constructive passion. Those who suffer from substance abuse possess self-destructive tendencies that damage their lives and affect the lives of their loved ones. Conversely, a runner's vitality transcends their own being and can have a positive effect on those around them.

Joanne and I woke early Tuesday morning to a magnificent, sunny day, hopped on the Harley and rode south through Townsend's Inlet, across the bridge below Ninety-forth Street to the neighboring town of Avalon. Along the main drag are a number of restaurants and we chose one with tables on a long outdoor porch. During breakfast I shared with her that I had been chronicling my training program for ten months in preparation for the Philly Marathon and considered translating the narrative into a book. Joanne responded, "You *are* a private person, aren't you? I can't believe you kept this to yourself for so long," and then followed with, "Cool, go for it." My most trusted agent endorsed my plan and told me to follow my dreams. She gave me all the encouragement I needed.

The timing to spend two weeks at the shore could not have been better. A series of strong ten-mile runs along the water's edge with the salt air spraying in my face and perspiration streaming from every pore of my body was a prescription for rejuvenation. The workouts were the type that drained tension from my body and mind, every thought was crystal clear and enthusiasm exuded when it was over. August in Sea Isle City was the first time I felt confident that I would conquer the 26.2 miles in November.

. . .

I returned to Cheltenham Village the last week in August physically, mentally and emotionally revived. Two weeks at the shore, complete with long runs, time with the family and the book germinating in my head was enough motivation to take training to the next level. Three weeks remained to prepare for the Distance Run, which I began with a strong eleven-mile run through Tookany Park the day we returned from the shore. I felt noticeably light on my feet for a day following a two-week vacation. Twenty years earlier I would have been sleeping off a hangover. It was a perfect start to another first—a scheduled forty-mile week. I needed to get past the half-marathon and begin pumping out longer distances that would begin with a fifteen-miler at the end of September.

Later in the week I went out for an eight-mile maintenance run and was heavy legged and unenthusiastic. I wondered what happened to the magic of the eleven-miler two days earlier, then I remembered I cut the lawn, worked in the garden, stacked about a half-cord of wood and cleaned the bathroom before I laced up the running shoes—plus it was ninety-five degrees with high humidity. I thought, What are the chances of a ninety-five degree day in November? and gave myself a break. I was psyched for a twelve-miler scheduled for the weekend.

. . .

The training program required a significant amount of time, energy and discipline. Most trainers recommend a program that climaxes with a twenty-mile run, a distance that typically requires training in excess of forty miles per week. Some trainers suggest closer to one hundred miles depending on an athlete's competitive level. Other factors that affect the quality of training include motivation, energy level, diet and adequate rest. Juggling such a demanding program with work, family and other commitments becomes a challenge for most recreational runners.

From time to time I'd question myself about the wisdom of my aspirations and wondered whether the time invested in the grueling regimen was worth the rewards. Though I enjoyed the fruits of good health, there were times it was difficult to rationalize running for hours on end, week after week—time that could have been spent with family and friends, or other constructive endeavors. I trained early in the morning and late in the evening as often as I could so it wouldn't interfere with family obligations. Still, sometimes I'd feel disengaged from Joanne and the kids. Alone with my thoughts one evening I wondered, *Is it worth it?*

An answer came unexpectedly during a morning run at the end of the month. I planned to run ten miles in preparation for the twelve-mile run on the weekend to cap off the forty-mile week. The ten-miler turned into the twelve-mile run and I entered a state of mind I hadn't visited in twenty years, the inimitable state referred to as *runner's high*.

Runner's high is a term exclusive to the running community. Athletes in other sports experience similar periods of enhanced performance that they refer to as *the zone* or *the flow*. Professional athletes spanning many sports attribute such performance to a heightened state of mind. The topic was studied in depth in the book *The Zen of Sports,* and explained as a phenomenon that sports psychologists describe as a buoyancy, an elevated sense of mastery and self-transcendence, and the absence of self-consciousness. Professional basketball players say the rim appears the size of a hula hoop when every shot they throw toward the net swishes through nothing but cotton, while batters say the baseball looks like a beach ball when they are able to hit any pitch a Major League pitcher throws to them. When runners reach such a state, the act of running becomes effortless and they feel as though their feet no longer touch the ground, as if they could go on forever.

No magic formula exists to attain a runner's high. There are no discrete number of miles or amount of hours that deliver a runner to the mystical state that transcends time and space. It has as much to do with persistence and commitment as it does the number of miles or hours, thus each runner experiences a different journey on his or her road to that level of consciousness. But one thing is certain: once in *the zone* a runner never wants to leave. It is a state of mind characterized as being uniquely in touch with one's spirit, and an experience that I believe sheds light on the words in the Book of Psalms, "Ye are Gods."

Ideally, remnants of the zone remain with a runner when both feet return to earth. The transcendent state introduces a more energetic life, optimistic outlook, improved relations and heightened clairvoyance. It is a stretch to say that even food tastes better and sleep is sounder, but that does appear to be true. Relationships with family and friends can improve when one party is more in tune with the world.

Distance runners spend countless solitary hours on the trail with endorphins emitting from the brain, which cultivates philosophical contemplation. Many testify they do their most creative thinking while on the trail. As I became more committed, running transcended phys-ical conditioning and opened my mind to appreciate life on a new and different level. Situations I'd experienced hundreds of times took on new meaning. When I looked into the eyes of people I'd known my entire life, it seemed as though I was more thoroughly connected. I felt present, though I never thought I was detached. Paradoxically, speeding up on foot slowed down my daily life and enabled me to connect. I was more attentive and inquisitive than usual when I read or researched for personal interest or business. I wanted to be a better mate, father, friend, boss and employee. I found a pureness in my being that I wanted to cling to and never let go.

When I came down from that magical twelve-mile run at the end of the month, I was certain that I would look back on it as my breakthrough run. It was oppressively humid and I was drenched, but not the least bit tired. In the midst of the run, I stopped at a tennis court at the end of the park, drank from the water fountain and threw cold water over my head and down the back of my neck to decrease my body temperature. The humidity lifted on the way back to the track and my energy surged. I added an additional mile and sprinted up the thirty-foot hill surrounding the track on each lap. On the final stretch along the trail I was euphoric, with Pearl Jam's "Corduroy" blasting through my headset, ". . . can't be what you want because I'm . . ." I would have run another five miles, but I wanted to see Colleen before she went downtown. The run was my second assurance in as many weeks that I would conquer 26.2 miles in November.

. . .

By September I was in intense training mode. Saturday, a week before the Distance Run, I decided I needed to push beyond thirteen miles. I psyched myself up during the week and was poised for the challenge. After work on Friday, I went with Dan to buy his first motorcycle and we celebrated at Taco Bell wolfing down tacos, not exactly the perfect training meal. I woke up Saturday morning intent on running fifteen miles, my first run to exceed a half-marathon distance in twenty years.

The run began pretty much as expected. The first few miles I wondered why the hell I ran at all, then after the five-mile mark the endorphins began to flow and I could think of nothing more invigorating than the cleansing physical, emotional and spiritual revival that awaited when I finished. Reality set in somewhere beyond mile thirteen and it hit me that I was only halfway to the distance I would run in November.

I hydrated every few miles and had taken a short breather before I set out on the final five-mile loop, but I didn't feel replenished. From out of nowhere, Mack appeared, as if by magic, and asked how I was doing. When I told him how I felt, he advised me to carry an energy drink anytime I attempted to run more than six miles. He also told me to carry an energy bar, fruit or other supplement to replenish potassium and other nutrients depleted during long-distance runs. I realized I was still a novice at endurance running and that a two-hour run had a much different effect on the body at forty-seven than it did at twenty-seven.

Twenty years earlier I never carried a water bottle—there was no G2, PowerShots or GU, only first-generation Gatorade. The days of running long distances unprepared were over and an education about proper diet, hydration and replenishment for endurance athletics began. The lesson helped me prepare for the Distance Run and the 25K Marathon Tune-Up more effectively than I had for any races in my life.

CHAPTER ELEVEN

STRANDED IN SEATTLE

Seattle left such lasting impression on my first visit in 1993 that I jumped at the opportunity to speak at a conference in September. The city is a rare American gem where you can stroll along a major seaport while captivated by views of majestic Mount Rainer and the Cascade Mountains to the Southeast and the Olympia Mountain Range to the West. It bustles with energy from the buzz of abundant coffee shops and restaurants, to its famous waterfront and the Public Market.

I arrived in Seattle mid-afternoon Monday, September 10th with a ticket for a return flight Wednesday morning. The early arrival allowed time for an afternoon run, so after I checked into the hotel a young man on the staff steered me down the road to the Mercer Slough Nature Park. The park had soft, winding trails around a pond and stream, boardwalks that spanned over water, and just enough hills to remind me of the fifteen miles I'd run two days earlier. The Distance Run was scheduled for Sunday and I planned only a few maintenance runs to stay limber through the week.

My internal clock still ticked to East Coast time Tuesday morning, and I had to force myself to stay in bed until five a.m. I couldn't lie still any longer, so I got up and went to the hotel gym for a workout before driving to our Seattle office. While my heart rate steadily climbed on the treadmill monitor, I watched a muted television overhead tuned to what I thought was a cheap "B" movie of an aircraft that had crashed into a tall office building. Then I recognized the small CNN logo on the corner of the screen and the singularly familiar skyline of New York City, and I realized I was watching live coverage of an aircraft that had torpedoed the World Trade Center's North Tower in Lower Manhattan.

I stepped off the treadmill just as someone walked into the gym. He read the bewildered look on my face, turned and his eyes locked onto the television, never saying a word. The camera shot was fixed on the two towers, one of them smoking from the upper floors, when a second aircraft came into view. It seemed to fly in slow motion, as if I could reach out and grab it before it smashed into the South Tower.

Shocked, I held onto the treadmill rail and watched in horror. Two symbols of American economic prowess and ingenuity were obliterated by two commercial airliners before day broke in Seattle. Wild thoughts raced through my head. *Thousands of aircraft take off and land in New York City airports each day without incident, so how could this be? What could explain two near-simultaneous catastrophes on a clear, sunny morning? It had to be an attack! My buddy Mike's wife worked in the North Tower, and she was there when it was bombed in 1993. Could she be lucky enough to escape two separate terrorist's attacks unharmed?*

By the time I got back to my room and turned on the television, the Pentagon had been hit by a third commercial airliner. Within another hour a fourth plane crashed into a field in western Pennsylvania, my home state. Both towers would collapse to the earth before I'd arrive at the office to begin the strangest workday of my career.

I had spent a lot of time in DC working for the Defense Department, but the second time in my life I'd travel to the state of Washington, the Pentagon, a building I visited regularly three thousand miles away in Virginia, was struck by an aircraft. The irony that I'd been in Washington state the year of the first World Trade Center bombing wouldn't hit me until much later.

Fort Lewis, the military base where I was scheduled to speak about the defense industrial base, was locked down and air travel was suspended. I was stranded in Seattle, a desirable place to be stranded under any other circumstances, but I needed to be with my family. We'd just emerged from a turbulent summer with Jimmy's health scare and started to regain stability at home, now I was thousands of miles away during the most horrific event of our lifetimes. Frivolous concerns about tuition bills, health insurance and work were now replaced by the prospects of terrorists' strikes and war. I wondered if the draft would be re-instituted, because I had three eligible sons. War seemed inconceivable since

America had been living in relative peacetime for so long, yet sitting in a hotel room in Seattle watching the slaughter of thousands of innocent people made war seem inevitable.

. . .

The days following September 11th, I booked two flights to Philly that were both canceled. Persistence paid off and I confirmed a seat on a Saturday morning flight home. I kept busy at our Seattle office and visited contractors to occupy my time. My buddy from our Seattle office, who had asked me to speak at the conference, invited me to his home for dinner on Thursday. I spent the evening with Bruce, his wife and children, a welcomed diversion from being stranded three thousand miles from home during the turmoil that swept the nation. After we finished dinner, Bruce took me for a ride up on a mountain to see the incredible Pacific Northwest scenery. He parked and we got out of the car to take a walk, when I heard a bagpipe in the distance. I looked down and saw a lone piper standing on the green of a golf course, the "Battle Hymn of the Republic" flowing from the cantor and drones of his instrument. If I didn't have a witness, I would have thought it was a dream.

During the week, whenever I looked outside my hotel window, I saw Mount Rainier in the distance, which seemed to be calling me. Early Friday morning I drove my rental car toward the fifth highest mountain in the Lower Forty-Eight. A snowcapped mountain in mid-September is a unique sight to an East Coast native, and the closer I got, the stronger the adrenalin pumped through my veins. As I rounded a curve along the park road, Rainier spanned the entire windshield and I followed signs leading to a lodge appropriately named Paradise. I stopped at the visitor center to pick up a trail map and honed in on Panorama Point, a trail near the highest elevation permitted without a guide or mountain climbing certification.

As I hiked up the trail, I was captivated by the vistas and began to understand how mountain climbers were lured to Everest and other majestic peaks around the world. I was sweating profusely at six thousand feet, and stress that had accumulated from the chaotic week oozed from my body. I had traveled across the country and climbed thousands of feet to experience the same sensation I grew to love when I took the long run.

When I approached the upper boundary of the hiking trail, I came across a man who appeared to be entranced by the scenery. I struck up a conversation with him and it became instantly apparent he was no stranger to the mountain. He treated me to a geology lesson and said, "Rainier is the best vantage point to see why they call these the Cascade Mountains. Follow that string of mountain peaks," he said, pointing south into the distance. "Do you see that peak sticking up way out there?" he asked.

"I sure do," I said.

"That's Mount Hood in Oregon. I climbed to the summit in 1981."

The year struck a chord—it was the same year I ran my first marathon. The excitement in his voice was contagious and I asked, "Do you mind if I ask your age?"

"Not at all," he said with a hint of swagger and a distinctive glimmer in his eye. "I'm eighty-one."

The math was easy. I was in the presence of an adventurer who climbed an 11,249-foot summit at the young age of sixty-one. I reached out, firmly held his forearm and said, "Please don't mind me. I need to hold you for a minute and get a transfusion of your energy and passion." He smiled.

After descending the trail, I drove back down the mountain and was lured to the side of the road by a spectacular waterfall. I no sooner got out of the car when a BMW motorcycle pulled into the parking space next to me. A couple who appeared well into their sixties dismounted and began removing their riding gear. The driver had a silver goatee, matching mid-length hair and a gold earring. His mate unzipped her leather jacket to expose a T-shirt decorated with a clown and the words "Clown Camp" inscribed. "Where did you folks travel from?" I asked.

"Orange County, California," the guy answered radiating a reserved energy. They brimmed with enthusiasm as they described their thousand-mile journey up the West Coast. I was inspired by the two seniors' zest for life, and couldn't help notice they had the same look in their eyes I'd seen an hour earlier in the elder adventurer's eyes at sixty-eight hundred feet.

On the ride back to the hotel it dawned on me that the adventurers I'd met that afternoon never uttered a word about the terrorists' attacks. The horrific events of the week were on every television and radio station, and in every newspaper. There was conversation about the attacks in every store, business or restaurant I'd entered; it was impossible to escape. Yet, these spirited adventurers seemed unscathed by the tragedy. I wondered whether an unbridled zest for life produced immunity to hate and evil.

Though stranded in Seattle the week of unprecedented mass murder on our soil, I learned irreplaceable lessons from three people much more experienced at life than myself. I always considered the seniors who lined up alongside me at races my heroes, but three seasoned adventurers on Mount Rainier drove the lesson home: regardless of age, there are no barriers to climbing an eleven thousand-foot summit or traveling one thousand miles on a motorcycle. And the glimmer in their eyes was all the proof I needed.

After traveling three thousand miles from home and climbing to almost seven thousand foot elevation, I finally figured it out. Every time I encountered someone with that distinctive "glimmer" in their eye, it was more than just a look. It was an energy, an aura with a captivating transference. It had nothing to do with age, sex, nationality, race, politics or interest—it had everything to do with passion. I'd found the key to detecting passion, and it held up every time.

. . .

Saturday morning I woke at three a.m. and drove to Sea-Tac Airport to wait four hours to process through increased security measures put in place before air travel resumed after the September 11th attacks. Tables were set up in the terminal where security personnel opened every piece of luggage and sifted through personal belongings. It was the beginning of a new reality. As if events of the week weren't stressful enough, after boarding the plane, and just when the flight attendant was about to secure the emergency door, there was an announcement to evacuate the aircraft. Security guards filed onboard with bomb sniffing dogs in response to a report of a suspicious package. Airport officials wouldn't unlock the terminal door, so roughly one hundred anxious passengers, many fidgety and some with panicked expressions on their face, were packed inside the claustrophobic tunnel between the plane and the terminal for over half an hour. The sole consolation from the ordeal was flying cross-country on what I considered the safest flight in history.

The plane arrived in Philadelphia late Saturday afternoon. I had forgotten until we landed that the Distance Run was the following day and pulled the race pamphlet from my bag. The deadline for picking up race packets with bib numbers and computer chips was six p.m. The clock on the dashboard read five-thirty. As I drove north on the Schuylkill Expressway, I called Joanne and told her I was back in Philly and would be home after I stopped downtown at the race expo to pick up my race packet. She was just happy I was back in town and replied, "Sure, babe!"

When I finally pulled into the driveway, it felt like I'd been gone for a year. Emotions ran high and hugs and kisses were flying everywhere. Extending the three-day trip to six days was a creative wardrobe challenge, nevertheless everyone was so relieved to be reunited that soiled clothes draped on a disheveled father and husband didn't interfere. First I embraced Joanne, lifting her off her feet and said, "Oh, I waited all week for this. It's so good to be home."

"I'm so glad you're back with us. I missed you so much," she said, holding me as though she'd never leave go.

The kids surrounded us and I reached out and pulled them into the scrum, "Boy, did I miss you guys." That began an exchange of stories about the emotional roller coaster ride we'd all been on during the unforgettable week. Sometime around midnight I made my way to bed. I was lucky if I got six hours' sleep before the Distance Run Sunday morning.

CHAPTER TWELVE

No Place Like Home

My head was in a fog when the alarm went off at six forty-five. I navigated the house trying to find the kitchen, poured a glass of orange juice, some of which wound up on the countertop, dropped a vitamin on the tile floor, bumped into a wall trying to find my keys and grabbed a banana for the road. Any advantage I thought I'd gain by packing the night before was wiped-out by my dazed condition.

The Jeep was in autopilot and dropped me off at the Wawa for some coffee. I sipped coffee and listened to a continuous stream of reports about the *Attack on America* all the way to the Broad Street exit of the expressway. I knew from experience there would be no parking spaces within a mile of the starting line, so I headed directly to Seventeenth Street just south of Spruce. A straggly homeless guy sitting against a stoned wall muttered to himself as I got out and took off my warm-ups, changed from flip-flops into New Balance and grabbed my bib. I smiled and said good morning, and he laughed and waved goodbye as I jogged to the starting line at Ninth and Market Streets. Billy Penn watched every step from his perch atop City Hall.

When I rounded the corner of Broad and Market Streets, a block-long line of portable toilets was a reminder that I'd overlooked my morning constitution. The advantage of being late for a race was that I didn't have to contend with five thousand people waiting to pee. I had a choice of stalls instead of having to find an alleyway; the only thing missing was the Sunday sports page. I drained my system in record time, catapulted from the stall and jogged to the starting line just before the gun sounded. Easing into the crowd of runners jamming Market Street, I pondered the sequence I'd just performed as a potential Olympic event.

A somber mood hung over the crowd during an emotional moment of silence. Rather than eardrum-reverberating rap, R&B or hard rock that usually kicks-off a long distance race, a singer bellowed "God Bless America" as runners filed past the starting line after the gun sounded. Many runners were dressed in patriotic garb. Red, white and blue shorts, shirts and bandanas were everywhere, and at least four runners carried Old Glory. A young man running next to me looked like a special operative, and I asked, "What branch of the service are you, buddy?"

"None sir, just a proud firefighter," he replied.

A drummer on the west side of the Falls Bridge that spans the Schuylkill River kept rhythm with the steady beat of runners' feet against asphalt, with the colors draped over his drums. On Kelly Drive a bagpiper in full Celtic garb played "The Battle Hymn of the Republic" with small American flags protruding from each of the pipes. The unwavering spirit of the American people was in full bloom. It was an emotionally charged race that led to my best half-marathon in years, finishing at 1:38:08, which ranked in the top twenty-five percent of my age group and twenty percent overall.

· · ·

Things changed drastically when I returned to work on Monday, as I expected working for the Defense Department. The office was operating twenty-four hours a day, seven days a week monitoring companies important to the national defense. I met with my boss to plan extended shifts to maintain around-the-clock coverage and I agreed to adjust my hours. It was the first time in years I'd worked a later shift, but I arrived in a better frame of mind because I was able to take a long morning run, which helped me cope with the chaos and stress.

I closed the books on September with an eighteen-mile run the last Saturday of the month. I left my work cell phone in the Jeep so I could disengage and when I returned two-and-a-half hours later I had twelve messages—so became my life. Nevertheless, it was the longest run I'd taken in twenty years and I felt strong and confident, though fully aware I was eight miles short of the marathon distance and still had unfinished business.

. . .

October rolled in and the marathon was no longer an abstraction or elusive event in the distant future—it was the following month! I prepared for a twenty-mile run the first weekend of the month as carefully as a freshwater fisherman plans for opening day of trout season in his favorite mountain stream.

The weatherman forecasted a torrential downpour with a twenty-degree drop in temperature. I went downstairs, had the usual juice and vitamin, grabbed an energy drink from the fridge, stretched and took off out the back door. Bracing myself for a chill, I ran into a seventy-degree wall of warm air. The first hour of the run was so humid I shed my long-sleeve tee and hat and threw them to the side of the Elkins Park track. After four miles around the quarter-mile track, I headed to Ogontz Field, roughly a mile through the small, hilly streets of Cheltenham, and ran another four miles before returning to Tookany.

By the time I got back to Elkins Park, the weatherman's redemption began with a heavy downpour. I ran another four miles around the track then headed down the parkway in what had turned into a monsoon. A heavy fog set in and visibility was near zero. When I got to the end of the parkway I was tempted to pack it in after seventeen miles, but with the race now six weeks away I knew I had to do the work. I willed myself through one more loop around the course to complete my first twenty-mile run in two decades. My sense of accomplishment overshadowed the pain that I knew awaited me when I woke Sunday morning, but I knew 26.2 would be a different animal.

The third Saturday in October I woke to the satisfaction that my final twenty-mile run would be behind me by noon. It was sixty-five degrees and damp when I stepped out the back door and got into the Jeep to drive to the Pine Road access to Pennypack Park. The morning sun shone through a light haze and caressed me while I stretched. I started out slow, feeling somewhat stiff, but once I got beyond five miles a good lather began to flow and a rhythm set in.

Approaching Holmesburg Prison at the halfway mark of the out and back course I passed a guy who looked vaguely familiar. I racked my brain trying to place his features, and it came to me that Joe was a character I cut my teeth with at the shipyard in what seemed another lifetime. On the rebound, our eyes made contact and it was obvious that I looked familiar to him as well, so I stopped. We made a futile attempt to catch up on the intervening years, babbling like two little kids. I started to cool down after a few minutes and explained I was in the middle of a twenty-mile run and if I didn't get moving I probably wouldn't finish. Joe was blown away that I was training for the Philly Marathon, especially since it was our first conversation in the absence of alcohol and other outlandish concoctions.

The brief encounter with my old buddy lifted my spirits and reminded me not to take health for granted, a tendency acquired from years of mingling with runners at long-distance races. Joe and I were close for a lot of years and he continued to live a wild lifestyle long after I got married. He almost lost a leg in a motorcycle accident. I was glad to see he was out and about walking among nature. The encounter made me realize that guys my age who still pounded the trails were the exception, which was reason enough to be grateful. With both the prison and Joe behind me, I was feeling spry. I gulped some Gatorade, bit off a piece of PowerBar and continued back to Pine Road.

October ended with the 25K Marathon Tune-Up along the River Drives. The out and back course travels west on Kelly Drive along the Schuylkill River, crosses the Falls Bridge and heads back toward the Art Museum on West River Drive before turning around just before the museum and backtracking. It was a crisp fall morning and although I didn't set a goal for the race, I ran strong and hit each mile mark under eight minutes, finishing in 2:01.

· · ·

The 25K was the last long run on the program before the marathon, but I reconsidered when the first week of November rolled around. As a novice, I was leery of going three weeks without a long run before the marathon, so the first Saturday of the month I set out for a seventeen-miler. I finished confidently and felt I made the right choice.

The final two weeks leading to the race I scaled back to short, maintenance runs between three and six miles. It was time to ease up on pounding my body and give it a chance to recover. The closer it got to the race, the more I wondered whether I'd make the distance—and if I did, would it be in a respectable time? I'd found the twenty-mile training runs grueling and questioned whether I'd be able to add another six miles the day of the race. The memory of "hitting the wall" somewhere around mile twenty-three in 1981 haunted me. Hitting the wall, also referred to as *bonking*, is a condition endurance athletes suffer when glycogen plummets, which weakens the muscles, and glucose drops, which shuts down the brain. When a runner hits the wall, it becomes increasingly difficult to function. *Would it happen again? And though I was able to run through the wall at age twenty-seven, would I be able to do it again at forty-seven?*

One fitful night about a week and a half before the race I couldn't sleep and got out of bed, went downstairs and popped open a Sierra Nevada Pale Ale. I sat chilling and downed another brew, feeling more relaxed than I had since turning up the training tempo during the summer. I realized that I fell back into the old trap—my existence revolved around nothing but logging miles on the trail. I'd forgotten how to disengage, so I made a decision not to take any runs longer than five miles before the race. The Harley got more miles on it than my running shoes did that final week, and an occasional beer disappeared from the fridge. It seemed I was on vacation, but a well-earned one.

After running injury-free for as long as I could remember, I woke up one morning with a pain that began in my right foot and traveled up into my shin. I couldn't believe it. Rather than do more damage, the weekend before the race my son Dan and I hopped on our motorcycles and rode to West Chester to see his brothers at college.

When we arrived, I followed Dan up a narrow driveway and into the parking lot behind Jay's apartment. We parked and got off our bikes just as a police car pulled up behind us. An officer squeezed his large frame out from behind the wheel. He first looked at the Harley, then Danny's Honda F-4, smirked and said to me, "You're riding with the wrong guy." It never occurred to me that we looked like the Odd Couple, Dan on a crotch rocket and me on a hog. We all laughed before he told us not to park in the lot without a permit, so we rode to the end of the alley and back onto the street. When we got to a stop sign Dan looked at me and said, "Where the hell are you going?"

"I'm looking for a parking spot."

Dan gave me an incredulous look as he pulled onto the sidewalk and parked. That moment was the first time it hit me that Dan was more like me than any of my other kids. He was independent yet compassionate, carefree yet sensitive. For so many years I agonized at the way we'd always butt heads, but it wasn't until Danny pulled onto the sidewalk and parked his motorcycle in West Chester that I realized it was because we were so much alike. Dan parked exactly where I would have parked when I was nineteen. I looked at him and laughed as I backed the Harley between two parked cars. Dan shook his head and laughed too.

. . .

The Sunday before the race I thought about all the training and sacrifice in my quest to run the Philly Marathon. I'd been diligent in my preparation, but was curious how I'd feel when I woke up November 18th to run the longest race since I was twenty-seven. The toll twenty years took on my body was a mystery that wouldn't unfold until hours after the starting gun sounded.

Colleen was college-hunting, and Sunday we drove to the University of Delaware. As we walked around campus, my right foot became increasingly sore, so I crossed running off my mental list of things to do later in the day. Monday was Veteran's Day and I dropped Joanne off at work, took my mom to breakfast then went back to her house and did a few chores. I stopped at Pep Boys on the way home and picked up supplies to change the oil and flush the radiator in the Jeep. It had been three days since I'd last run and I was beginning to get a case of runner's guilt, so I split some wood and hit the heavy bag in the back of the garage before going into the house. I completely abstained from any type of training on Tuesday and worked out with light-weights on Wednesday. Four days until the marathon and I hadn't run in almost a week. I was restless, but ignored the temptation to run, convinced that my body would be thankful on Sunday. After logging between thirty and forty-mile weeks for months, I was about to conquer my longest run in twenty years with zero miles on the pedometer the final week.

I broke down on Thursday and decided to test my sore foot with a short three miler. There was some pain during the run, but it felt better as the day progressed. I went for a short two-mile run before work on Friday with no discomfort. After work I mixed it up with light-weight training, hitting the heavy bag and a two miler just to stay limber. I felt healthy and decided that was it, no more running until the starting gun on Sunday morning.

Nearly a year had passed since the idea of running the marathon had entered my feeble mind, and I woke up the day before the race excited. Arriving at the point where I was fit enough to attempt such a challenge was immeasurably satisfying. After all that I put myself through—the blood, sweat and tears—I swore to myself that nothing would stop me from conquering the marathon the following morning.

Saturday night I gathered the running gear I would take when I woke Sunday morning. Preparation was so uncharacteristic for a disorganized soul like me that I laughed thinking about how important the race must be to plan such detail. I even packed clothes to change into after the race. It was so un-me. At eleven o'clock I hit the sack, missing "Saturday Night Live" for the first time in memory.

CHAPTER THIRTEEN

PHILLY MARATHON 2001

I woke early Sunday morning to beautiful fall weather befitting the challenge I'd prepared for since my epiphany in Old Town. The sun was blinding, temperature brisk, and not a trace of humidity or wind—ideal marathon conditions. I wandered downstairs, chased a vitamin with orange juice and made a pot of coffee.

The moment seemed surreal. I thought how fast the year went—training, races, conditioning during the humid summer months, fatigue, sacrifice. Now I sat in my kitchen and looked out the window at a beautiful November morning eager to run 26.2 miles. The memory of crossing the finish line at my first marathon on a Sunday morning in 1981 made me smile.

I was so preoccupied during the ride to center city that I never thought Kelly Drive would be closed until after I exited the expressway at Ridge Avenue. I detoured through Fairmount Park to Thirty-third Street, then down side streets to finally make my way across from the Philadelphia Museum of Art. The clandestine parking spots I'd discovered years earlier on Pennsylvania Avenue adjacent to the defunct railroad tracks were filled, obvious victims of time and word of mouth. One side of the street was jammed, the other side had a No Parking sign that I didn't bother to read, and was empty. I figured, screw it! and parked on the empty side. By the time I got out and walked to the end of the block, the Jeep was wedged between parked cars that filled the entire length of the street. I would be safe from being towed.

The front of the Art Museum was filled with anxious runners imitating Rocky, running up the steps and stretching. Once I was limber I went to relieve myself a final time before the starting gun. The long lines to the Port-O-Potties were out of the question, so I joined the bohemians in the park across the street. After emptying my tank, I jogged back to the starting line, got a bottle of water and stretched some more before I took my place among nearly four thousand runners.

My adrenalin pumped harder when the master of ceremonies took the microphone, asked for a moment of silence for the victims and families of the September 11th attacks, and then introduced a student from a local elementary school who sang the national anthem. By the time the young girl finished, the runners were brimming with anticipation. Many were preoccupied in their pre-race rituals; some running in place, some stretching, while others were absorbed in meditation. We wished one another the best of luck, patted each other on the back and exchanged small talk. Suddenly, a gun blast rang out starting a stampede through the City of Brotherly Love.

The herd ran shoulder-to-shoulder east on Benjamin Franklin Parkway, rounded Logan Circle and headed back toward the Art Museum before making a right on Arch Street to Penn's Landing. It took the field of four thousand several miles to thin out as runners vied for position in the narrow canyon sandwiched between tall buildings. The course turned south along the Delaware River before cutting over to Front Street. I came upon a runner with a message written on the back of her T-shirt, "First Marathon, Prayers Accepted," and told her my prayers were with her, but to please reciprocate. She obliged.

Smiling volunteers directed the pulsating mass west onto South Street and into Center City. Somewhere around mile six I approached a tall, lean runner with a shaved scalp who looked like a Marine, carrying the American flag. I offered to lighten his load for a mile or two and he said, "No thanks, but ask again around mile twenty."

I said, "If you're still running this pace at mile twenty, I'll be too far behind to offer, buddy."

The course bisected Downtown to Thirty-fourth Street through the Drexel University campus, and then made a right turn through Powelton Village. Enthusiastic revelers who appeared as though they'd partied through the night were yelling, drinking and high-fiving runners as they passed through their neighborhood. One inebriated woman offered slugs of wine from her bottle. I declined and told her, "Too early, honey, see me at mile twenty-four."

Music blared in the distance after I passed the Philadelphia Zoo at Girard Avenue, where Thirty-fourth Street turns into Lansdowne Drive. A steady stream of fans formed on the side of the winding road that climbs the hill to Memorial Hall, where volunteers and spectators handed out fruit and drinks. At mile marker ten I was surprised when I saw a digital clock that revealed I was running a sub eight-minute mile pace, exceeding my expectations. The course veered right onto Belmont Avenue and back into Fairmount Park when I sensed a slight pain in my right foot; otherwise I felt remarkably strong.

The course followed Black Road down behind Memorial Hall, and finally dumped the runners onto West River Drive under a canopy of trees, many shedding their flaming auburn leaves onto the ground. The scenic part of the race had just begun. An out-of-town runner next to me commented about the beauty, pointing across the river to Boathouse Row, Water Works and the cascading waterfall, which reminded me how fortunate I was to run the course whenever the urge struck. Closing in on the fifteen-mile mark another clock indicated I was still maintaining close to an eight-minute-mile-pace at 2:01, roughly the time I finished the 25K a few weeks earlier. I couldn't help think that I could possibly beat my 1981 finishing time of 3:34 if I maintained the pace. I was excited, but knew adrenalin would carry me only so far.

I'd followed all the conventional training methods for endurance racing and was confident. Several days before the race, I increased my carbohydrate intake, a process known as "carb loading." Carbohydrates are the body's main energy source and by increasing their consumption before an endurance event an athlete can store more energy in their muscles to increase stamina and avoid fatigue. I also hydrated with energy drinks before and during the race, and stored energy gels, concoctions packed with carbohydrates, potassium and other nutrients, in my pockets to consume during the race.

The brief moment of euphoria evaporated as my condition rapidly deteriorated on Kelly Drive. By mile sixteen my left knee began to tighten, something I hadn't encountered on any of the long training runs. By mile seventeen the tightening evolved into a sharp pain that forced me to the side of the road where I squatted to compress the knee joint as far as it would allow. The compression relieved the tightness, if only temporarily. I pressed on, but the tightening persisted and required periodic stretching that affected the pace I'd maintained the first fifteen miles. The pain was a stark reminder of reality, and my focus shifted to finishing.

The crowds from East Falls to Manayunk provided a well-needed shot of motivation. Around mile eighteen, people yelled wildly and held up signs encouraging the runners, as a bagpiper in Celtic garb stood playing at the head of the Falls Bridge. Hundreds of screaming fans spilled from the curbside into the streets, high-fiving runners as they entered Manayunk. Main Street, so narrow a drunk could spit from one sidewalk to the other, was crammed with spectators three and four deep the entire length. People offered bananas, oranges and Jell-O shots to take the runners' minds from the agony their bodies endured.

The turnaround point was a welcome sight at the end of Main Street, the twenty-mile mark. Retreating from Manayunk, I thought I was hallucinating when I saw an oasis—a beer station. Guys and gals staged a long wooden table, the top covered with cups filled with cold beer for runners who were so inclined—I double fisted. The beer station was the first I'd encountered during a distance race, and I prayed it wouldn't be the last. As I made my way back down Kelly Drive with Manayunk's energy infused in my body, the crowd in East Falls seem louder than when I passed earlier.

Memories of the1981 Philadelphia Independence Marathon began to torment me. *My thighs were in an incendiary rage as though covered with napalm and I thought my calves would explode and splatter blood all over spectators lining Kelly Drive.* Though I was suffering physically, I invested twenty-two miles and swore I would will myself to the finish line. Nothing would deny me of finishing the race. Nothing!

I was in no-man's land, somewhere within those "Six Miles of Truth," where the race transforms from a physical endurance challenge to a psychological test of a runner's mettle. Training, carb loading, energy gels, hydration, music and crowds can get a runner to mile twenty, but only single-minded determination deliver a marathoner to the finish line. By the twentieth mile an endurance runner is stripped of ego and left naked. Loud music and cheers are ineffective, unflagging resolve and raw tenacity are essential—but no guarantee.

Halfway back down Kelly Drive I thought about my Friday routine when I worked in South Philly, when I would change into running gear in the office and stop to run the 8.4-mile River Drive loop to begin the weekend. It became my favorite running trail in the city, one I would go out of my way to visit whenever I had business in town. I closed my eyes and envisioned the finish line in front of the museum steps.

My pain subsided when a tall, pretty blonde with two deformed arms passed me at mile twenty-five. The young girl's courage inspired me for the final push to the finish and reminded me of the truly gallant athletes that conquer a 26.2-mile course. I was embarrassed to succumb to leg pain and pressed on.

Closing in on the Art Museum with Boathouse Row to my right, I knew I would make it. As I eased up the incline in the final quarter mile, I peeped over the horizon and saw the side of Billy Penn's head amid the city skyline. I followed the bend in the road and looked up to my right at the museum steps where Rocky Balboa trained for his title fight with Apollo Creed. I wasn't moving as fast as Rocky, but I was still standing.

Thousands of screaming spectators greeted the exhausted runners as music thundered through huge speakers. Families and friends greeted their runners as they passed under a large yellow banner and crossed the finish line, expressing admiration for their achievement. I was fresh and confident when I left a crowd at the starting line, and returned nearly four hours later choking back tears—tears of raw emotion that climaxed nearly a year of training. When my feet hit the cushion covering the sensors at the finish line, from out of nowhere I broke down and cried.

In 1981, my Dad and Joanne, with Jimmy and Jason in strollers, watched as I crossed the finish line on Chestnut Street after my first marathon. Now, Dad was gone and Joanne shuffled our four kids between soccer games and gymnastics meets, and I was greeted by strangers. Though my loved ones weren't present, I felt connected as if they were right next to me, our bond so strong it transcended time and space. So much had changed in twenty years, yet for some reason I was pulled back to the marathon.

I struggled to stoop and remove the computer chip from my laces. The chip records a runner's official time when it passes over electronic sensors at the finish line. My chip joined thousands of others in a cardboard box. A day later I learned the sensor at the finish line registered 3:56:19 from the chip I wore on my shoe.

. . .

I sat on the side of a fountain at the base of the Art Museum in the warm fall afternoon sun washing down a cup of hot soup with a cold beer, an Irishman's brunch. I pondered whether the epiphany in Old Town was an errant, misguided idea that gained momentum like a good intention that went awry. My body was beat up, run down and bruised— a reminder why I hadn't run a marathon in twenty years. An internal debate bounced around inside my head whether the benefits from the conditioning program outweighed the foot injury and nagging pain at the base of my neck; they were injuries I hadn't experienced in a lifetime of running shorter distances. I struggled to determine if neglecting other things I enjoyed in exchange for running the marathon was worth the effort and sacrifice. After the initial euphoria dissipated, I reconciled that I made the correct decision twenty years earlier and renewed the vow to never run another—at least not for another twenty years.

Though I was pleased with the achievement of running a marathon at the age of forty-seven, I felt a void when I thought about what I'd do next. My thoughts turned to more practical goals, but regardless the challenge, I was determined never to change. I believed slowing down would only begin an atrophy, so never slowing down became a goal in itself.

Ten months earlier I was captivated by the harebrained idea that it would be cool to run my second marathon twenty years after my first, a goal that preoccupied my life for nearly a year. A sane person would consider such an ambition preposterous; perhaps explained only by using a mountain climber's analogy, "Because it's there." I smiled whenever I'd reflect on the memories of the training runs and the races; and that I had joined a small percentage of folks my age that conquered the 26.2-mile feat. But the real reward was the contentedness that I craved—at least initially.

After crossing the finish line I swore my marathon career would be capped at two, but twenty years earlier I swore I'd never run another. In the months that followed the race I was still noncommittal, but eased up on the swearing. More moderate distances like 10Ks and ten-milers down Broad Street were likely. The Distance Run, well, maybe. But a marathon? I just didn't know. The commitment, wear and tear on the body, and sacrifice caused me pause. Maybe I'd feel different in another twenty years—just maybe.

CHAPTER FOURTEEN

ONLY THE BEGINNING

After dedicating nearly one year to training for a marathon at a stage in life when most my friends were concentrating on either improving their golf game or looking to upgrade to a carbon fiber frame for their bike, I was motivated to convert my chronicles into a book to share my experience with others, but I struggled to find a message that would resonate and couldn't write the final chapter. I became frustrated that I was unable to translate an experience that moved me so profoundly into a meaningful story. Every time I reviewed my notes I'd cringe at the thought that it would sound like another boring account about some self-absorbed jock, well past his prime, who ran a marathon. Big deal! Something was missing.

The spunk that had eluded me since the end of November reemerged and I decided not to allow the impasse with the book to interfere with setting a fitness goal for 2002. I was still indifferent about attempting another marathon, but was intrigued with an idea to compete in a triathlon. An Ironman Triathlon, which consists of a 2.4-mile swim, 112-mile cycle and 26.2-mile race, was out of the question. Its little brother, the Olympic Triathlon, a 1.5K swim, 40K cycle and a 10K run, would be a comparative walk in the park. I swam each week with the Special Olympics as a volunteer swim coach, cross-trained on the mountain bike and ran routine 10Ks. Cycling and running came naturally and would be a cinch, but I'd always found swimming a cardiovascular challenge.

Within a few weeks, the triathlon fascination subsided and I abandoned the goal. I'd been through the euphoria enough times to acknowledge it was in my DNA to get all worked up over a new goal, especially a physical challenge. I wondered whether physical endurance goals were camouflaging more deeply-rooted issues. Was I running for my health or was I running away from digging deeper within to find out what I was all about? If life is a journey, I was unlikely to find its meaning in a one-year training program.

Running is a solitary endeavor and inherently conducive to introspection. I'd sought the solitude of the trails throughout my lifetime to figure out the solution to dilemmas I encountered with my family, job or life in general, so I decided to be patient and allow the message of my chronicles to germinate along the trail.

The year progressed uneventfully—work, Broad Street Run, soccer games, 10Ks, business travel, the Distance Run, gymnastics meets, ice hockey tournaments, birthdays and paying the bills—well, maybe not so uneventfully. When October rolled around an application for the 25K Marathon Tune-Up appeared in the mail. I was powerless to the cheap fifteen dollar registration fee that included a long-sleeve tee. I registered on an impulse. The Distance Run had been my longest run the entire year, about five miles short of the Marathon Tune-Up. My only expectation was to finish.

The morning of the race, the temperature was about sixty degrees, not a trace of humidity or cloud in the sky as I ran along West River Drive, when a young guy appeared alongside me who didn't seem to be in the race. We exchanged small talk before he told me he was training to run his first marathon, then he shared advice his brother had given him. He called it the three-hour theory—replacing a twenty-mile training run with a three-hour run. It was the first alternative I'd heard to the conventional marathon-training rule of thumb, which advises runners to work up to a twenty-mile training run before attempting a marathon. Twenty miles is roughly three-quarters the distance of a marathon; however three hours was not as finite because marathoners finish at different times—it was more flexible. I liked flexible, so it made perfect sense to me.

I ran strong the entire race and finished within five minutes of my time from a year earlier even though my training paled in comparison. The 25K taught me that one-size training program doesn't fit all. Each athlete has a different body structure, metabolism, bone density, and so on, and running long distances for months at a time didn't seem to be the best training philosophy for my body. The rigorous training program

I followed in 2001 pounded my aging body into oblivion, and I was hampered by injury before the race even began and wound up at the doctor's office a few days after it was over. In 2002, I trained with only a few mid-range runs, alternated with cycling, and ran the 25K within five minutes of my finishing time of a year earlier—the best part was that I was injury-free. My experience was confirmation to Doctor Sheehan's theory that, "We are each an experiment of one."

I assessed how my body held up in the 25K with less-intensive training and reconsidered my strategy, and then reneged on a vow I'd made to myself a year earlier. I figured I could prepare for a marathon with only a few additional long runs and end the training program with a three-hour run—advice from the novice on West River Drive. I felt stronger and more confident when I entered the 2002 Philly Marathon than the previous year, mainly because I wasn't hampered by injury.

Two weeks before the marathon, Jo and I drove to the University of Scranton to visit Colleen for family weekend. Though the weekend schedule was full, I managed to squeeze in an hour run on the mountain roads of northeastern Pennsylvania. It was a holiday weekend and I planned to take the three-hour run on Monday.

Early Monday morning I drove to Valley Green and ran Forbidden Drive in Fairmount Park toward Kelly Drive with GUs in both pockets and a buoyant stride. It seemed I'd barely begun the run when I crossed Ridge Avenue onto Kelley Drive. I ran across the Falls Bridge and effortlessly down West River Drive toward the Art Museum. I crossed back over the Schuylkill River and passed the Waterworks and then Boathouse Row. At the end of the River Drives, I left civilization behind and reentered Forbidden Drive. Two hours into the run and immersed in perspiration, I noticed that the gentle beat of my heart and the soft panting of breath in and out of my lungs were in perfect harmony with my stride. I checked the time as I approached Valley Green and still had a half-hour remaining, so I continued to Northwestern Avenue at the end of the trail and turned around. Out of GUs and somewhat weary, I was pleased with how strong I felt when I finished, especially since I'd exceeded the three hours by fifteen minutes. I had that good runner's soreness, but not the nagging pain I'd experienced after twenty-mile long runs in past years. Maybe it was psychological, or maybe the cumulative impact of too many long runs wore my body down in the past. I didn't know, and I didn't care. Though I was short of the time it would take to run the marathon, experience told me that the adrenalin, the crowd and my fellow runners could get me to the finish line.

The night before the race I sat in my basement reminiscing about past races—my first Broad Street Run in 1980, the 1981 Philadelphia Independence Marathon and countless Broad Street and Distance Runs that I'd run with family and friends. Somehow, 2002 seemed different. It was therapeutic. Work had become increasingly stressful and the long, draining runs were cathartic. I would push beyond my endurance threshold and find solace on the other side of exhaustion. I had registered for the 2002 marathon on a whim and wound up totally into it.

I woke up Sunday morning confident and motivated. I snuck out the back door, drove downtown and illegally parked not far from the Art Museum. With no time to warm up, I nudged my way into the crowd of runners while the National Anthem played over the loud speakers. The gun sounded and it was off to the races with Green Day's "Basket Case" blasting through my headset.

I measured my progress against memories from the 2001 marathon. Rather than struggling past Memorial Hall at mile eleven, I whizzed by with fresh legs and all but danced down the hill on Black Road onto West River Drive. Rounding the Art Museum onto Kelly Drive at mile fifteen, I settled into a comfortable rhythm and recalled the spot I first broke down in 2001. As my confidence grew, I increased the pace to exorcise the painful memories from a year earlier. The rowdy Manayunk crowd provided the usual lift, especially the reliable barkeeps manning the beer table, where I double fisted once again. I felt fresher with 10K remaining than I had at the same point during my first two marathons. I shed my shirt at mile twenty-two, sucked down a final PowerGel and turned up the headset for the homestretch.

My adrenalin pumped as I passed Lloyd Hall, and I picked up the pace approaching the hill leading to the Art Museum. I was running faster than I had the previous six miles. When I stepped over the finish line at 3:58:52, I was revived—sore, for sure, but revived. I grabbed a few PowerBars, bananas, bagels and soup, and washed it all down with a couple of cold beers.

. . .

I sat at the foot of the museum steps and grinned thinking how I'd just finished the same course within a few minutes of the time I had run a year earlier, with only a fraction of the training and not nearly as much pain. The experiment was a success and my new training strategy proven—I concluded that I had over-trained in 2001. My body was no longer able to endure forty-mile training weeks for months on end without consequence. Rather than strengthening my body, sixteen weeks of pounding had beaten it to a pulp. One year after I had suffered along the exact same course, I finished drained, but exhilarated and injury-free, with that good sore a runner savors. It was the kind of soreness that reminds a healthy body it can be pushed to extreme limits, yet recover to face another challenge.

At the young age of forty-eight I had a lot to be thankful for. There were daily reminders that health is not something to be taken for granted. Walking down the street, in the workplace, even lying on the beach were constant reminders of the many forms of creation. I considered myself fortunate and vowed to run for as long as I was able. It was the least I could do.

When 2003 rolled in, I upped the ante and set a goal to run two marathons. The Ocean Drive Marathon in early March began in Cape May, New Jersey, and ended on the boardwalk in Sea Isle City. My brother Jack, who had followed my running antics for years, volunteered to join me and represented my one-man fan base. We drove down the night before the race and went to the Ugly Mug Tavern in Cape May. Jack sat across from me and broke my balls while I loaded up on carbohydrates and generally made a pig of myself. It was exactly what I needed to loosen up for marathon.

My streak of excellent weather conditions on race day was wiped out by a Nor'easter with relentless rain blowing off the ocean, seemingly sideways much of the race. I'd been advised that the weather at previous Ocean Drive Marathons had been horrible, but naturally ignored the warnings and dressed as though I was going for a five-mile run through the park in April, wearing a long sleeve tee, light-weight running pants and a baseball cap. Usually bare-chested at the end of a marathon, I was waterlogged and nearly frozen in clothes that weighed an extra five pounds by the time I reached JFK Boulevard in Sea Isle City. Jack watched me spin deliriously down the boardwalk and cross the finish line at 3:53:47.

My body and brain required an hour in the hot tub and a substantial amount of alcohol to thaw. I began thinking about where I'd run the second marathon of the year and narrowed it down to two venues, Philly or Steamtown in Scranton, PA. Both had advantages, Philly for the convenience of the home turf and Steamtown for speed and beauty. There was still plenty of time to decide. Then my thoughts turned to 2004 when I would celebrate my fiftieth birthday. It didn't seem that long ago I swore I'd never run another marathon. Now I considered running three the year I would become a half-centenarian.

CHAPTER FIFTEEN

TEAR AND REVIVAL

I celebrated my forty-ninth birthday in July. The point at which I joined the ranks of the middle-aged was muddled. It was as though one day I emerged from a decades-long fog with hair missing from my head that relocated to my torso, and I was indifferent to both. I wandered through those years oblivious to the role running played in my life.

I was lying around in the family room with the kids on a brutally hot July 4th weekend, when Joanne walked in and told me her car wouldn't start. Naturally, the car was blocking the other cars in the driveway, so I helped the boys push her Nissan up the incline and onto the street. Mindlessly, I wore a pair flip flops to push the car—that was my first mistake. Later that evening, soreness developed in my left knee and I thought about how my feet slid around inside the flip flops as I pushed the car. The pain got worse as the night wore on. My second mistake was continuing to run on the sore knee. I took a day or two off, but didn't allow enough time for the knee to recover. Rather than visit an orthopedic specialist, I sought the advice of my family doctor, who prescribed the equivalent of taking two aspirin and a call-back in the morning. The third mistake was entering Captain Bill's Beach Run, a ten-mile race in Sea Isle City, New Jersey. Three strikes and you're out. I hobbled through the second half of the race and was so sore when it was over, I could barely push down the clutch to shift gears on the drive home. The following week I did what I should have done in early July and went to the orthopedic doctor. After an evaluation and MRI, he told me I had a torn meniscus that required arthroscopic surgery.

Stupidity obliterated my 2003 goal for the second marathon, but I'd been a bonehead my entire life, so I was well-conditioned for the blow. Reality set in when the doctor suggested I consider limiting future races to 5K or 10K, and definitely not longer than a half-marathon. His advice sent shock waves through my thick head. I'd almost made it to fifty without ever giving a thought to limiting any type of physical activity, and I generally ignored people who suggested that I begin acting my age. Now here I was being told by an orthopedic surgeon to change my ways, and was dubious whether I'd be capable of gently easing into midlife once I was off the injured reserve list. I just couldn't picture myself trading an active lifestyle for a round of shuffleboard or game of bocce while decked out in a pair of plaid Bermuda shorts and a white, tweed hat.

A meniscus tear is not an uncommon injury for an athlete; however it won't improve the performance of a forty-nine year old runner with early stages of arthritis. Nevertheless, tearing my meniscus came with an ironic twist of fate. I'd become a twelve-month runner and hadn't taken time off from the sport in years; everything I did revolved around running. Now, for the first time since letting go of the coffee table as a toddler I was unable to run. I joined a gym to rehab my knee and began a bona fide weight training routine, something I hadn't done since high school. My legs became stronger from leg presses, curls and extensions, toe lifts, and working out on the stationary cycle and elliptical machine. I was bench pressing the weight I had when I was a youth and added muscle to my frame. I also became serious about mountain biking. When I stepped back and evaluated my fitness from a new perspective, I realized I felt healthier than I had when I was in peak running condition.

Following doctor's orders, I refrained from running until January of 2004. I began on the treadmill, alternating between walking and a slow jog to begin toughening up the repaired cartilage. It took several weeks to work up to a mile, an accomplishment I would have considered embarrassing in the past, but an achievement I was now excited about.

I entered my first 10K roughly four months after knee surgery when I found out Brian's Run had been snowed-out in December and rescheduled to late March. The run through West Chester and the surrounding countryside was the first test on the repaired knee, but the most satisfying part of the day was meeting Brian, the race's namesake, after the race. A paraplegic confined to a wheelchair for decades, Brian exuded so much happiness it was impossible to not be inspired. His bright smile remained with me when I departed, and I realized the insignificance of a torn meniscus in the grand scheme of things.

Meeting Brian refreshed my outlook and taught me there was more to life than running. I challenged myself to channel the effort I dedicated to the sport of running into something tangible that would contribute to society, which became fundamental to transforming my narrative.

The realist in me knew that I'd be out on the trails for years to come, yet I craved more than fitness and contentment from my effort. I developed a desire to form a message that would resonate with everyday recreational runners, as well as those on the sidelines curious whether they should lace up a pair of running shoes or go for a walk. I had crossed paths with people from all walks of life that reaped benefits from their particular passion no different than the benefits I got from running. Then it struck me—running was my gig. I needed to translate my chronicles into a narrative with a message that would inspire people to be active and help them find fulfillment and contentment in their lives.

. . .

There was no indication Brian's Run would be the beginning of my most prolific year as a runner. The March 10K was motivation to register for the Penn Relays Distance Classic in April. It would be the first time in my life I would run 20K before the Broad Street Run in May.

The Penn Relays is the first and largest track and field event in the world, with a history dating back to 1895. The Distance Classic is a 20K that kicks-off the carnival of track and field competition the Sunday before the official opening ceremony. I'd attended the relays twice as a spectator while Colleen was in high school to watch her compete on the same track as world-class runners. I'd never followed the sport closely, and was familiar with names like Jumbo Elliott and Ron Delany only because they were local legends. By the time I would run on the track at Franklin Field I was more knowledgeable about their accomplishments, all the teams that Coach Elliott led to victory and that the venerable Ron Delany's name was inscribed on the Wall of Fame inside the stadium. That I would set foot on the same track as these legends raised goose bumps all over my body.

The sun was blinding in a cloudless sky outside Franklin Field. The starting gun sent runners north on Thirty-third Street before the course cut through the narrow city streets of Powelton Village lined with row homes, crossed over the Schuylkill River and made a U-turn onto West River Drive. I felt strong and kept pace alongside members of the Philadelphia Freedom Striders running club, but began feeling the effects of the four-month layoff when I crossed the Falls Bridge near the turnaround point on Kelly Drive.

I began running out of steam after mile ten and struggled past the Art Museum just before the mile eleven marker. The rush from the crowd on Thirty-first Street back in Powelton Village was just enough to carry me back to Franklin Field. Approaching the bend leading to the starting line outside the stadium, I gave what little kick I had remaining only to find that the finish line was another few hundred yards inside the stadium. I ran the final quarter mile in the glistening sun around the same track on which I had watched Colleen compete.

The following month I toed the line with Jimmy and his buddy Shawn, along with more than twelve thousand runners for the twenty-fifth annual Broad Street Run. I'd never logged so many races by the beginning of May in any year my entire life, and it only took six months to violate my orthopedic surgeon's advice to limit my running to shorter distances.

. . .

The following week I was in a running shoe store and a registration form for a half-marathon promoted as, "The Feat in the Heat," grabbed my attention. I filled out the form and mailed in my check before I realized I'd registered for my first trail run. Memorial Day weekend Ed and I would drive to Plowville, PA, to run the Charlie Horse Half Marathon Trail Run.

Trail running is an experience like none I'd encountered in all of the years of pounding the concrete and asphalt. Though many of my running routes were off-road, they were tame trails in parks or on cinder or synthetic tracks. I got an early indication this would be a completely different experience when volunteers herded us onto a school bus for the ride to the starting line. As the bus snaked through the forest, climbed mountains and descended valleys, I realized I was in for a challenge beyond what I'd bargained for. It didn't take long before my suspicions were confirmed.

The half-marathon course was a continuum of trails cut through desolate woods, towering hills, narrow streams and downed-trees, with no option other than reaching the finish line. Before we were a mile into the race, we climbed two near-vertical hills, ran through a creek and scurried narrow paths filled with rocks and boulders. I had expended the equivalent of a 10K's energy and still had eleven miles to go. Before I got to the first water station, my foot caught a rock and sent me flying head-first into the brush. I rolled and sprung back to my feet with a different outlook on trail running. If the race hadn't been so much fun, I would have questioned my sanity for spending the holiday weekend punishing myself in such a manner.

I crossed the finish line disheveled, cut, bruised, with an aching ribcage, and an ear-to-ear, shit-eating grin. I officially claimed the knee was completely rehabilitated and knew I could rely on it for more serious challenges. After the race I learned the event benefited the Berks County chapter of the Special Olympics, which made the bodily sacrifice worth every laceration. The Charlie Horse trial run marked a new chapter in my running life.

. . .

The trail run hook was set, and the following month Ed and I drove west to French Creek State Park at eight a.m. on another Sunday morning. This time it was the Double Trouble, a trail run with an option to register for either a 15K or 30K, but with a twist. Runners who registered for the 15K and felt spunky when they got to the finish line could continue for a second loop for the 30K. Conversely, runners who registered for the 30K and came to their senses at 15K had the option of changing their planned halfway point to the finish line. Go figure.

I was a little overzealous and went for the 30K, averaging roughly one fall per 10K. The last fall was pretty spectacular and if not for a large rock, I likely would have rolled another twenty feet down an embankment. Luckily the rock was round, so I didn't puncture a lung, which would have slowed me down considerably. I was sore for a week and couldn't roll over on my back while sleeping at night. It required Oscar-worthy acting to conceal from Joanne that her middle-aged mate was wounded playing in what she would likely consider a playground for adults who refused to grow up.

Trail running is completely different from road racing and requires strategic adjustments. Its unique aspects are discovered only from experience—a literal school of hard knocks. Trails can be strewn with obstacles that require deliberate footwork to avoid hidden rocks, camouflaged vines and rambling streams, all of which are threats to straining a groin muscle or quad, not to mention broken bones. Road races are absent such obstacles. The chances of tripping over a boulder or log while running down Broad Street are somewhat remote.

When the dizziness subsided, I realized I'd crossed the finish line at 3:18 and wondered how I ran at such a slow pace. It took several trail runs to realize that the correlation between the finishing time for a road race and that of a trail run was like comparing apples and rotten bananas. No formula exists to compensate for the time spent climbing hills, rolling on the ground, pulling limbs and stones out of shoes or helping fellow-runners out of the brush. I acclimated to the slower time when I realized I finished in the top fifteen percent of the field; a couple of races nearly breaking the top ten finishers in my age group. Best of all, I felt stronger, like I had a more thorough workout, after I finished a trail run, compared to how I felt after running road races my entire life.

. . .

It took only two trail runs to figure out the sport attracted its share of eccentric athletes. These runners' wore their hair a bit longer, a few more faces were unshaven, and bare-chested runners were more common (male runners, of course). The parking lot had less BMW's and more SUV's; and noticeably more bike and kayak racks, and off-beat and obscene bumper stickers. The crowd was more gregarious, less uptight and livelier after the race. There was also evidence that most had been weaned from those tasteless light beers. I felt more at home among the trail runners.

The race organizer operated out of Reading, Pennsylvania and created unorthodox wilderness courses in the middle of nowhere that sometimes included an alternative water station in the late miles of the race stocked with beer. Finishers received an obligatory reward for their suffering, such as a beer glass with an outlandish race insignia inscribed on the side.

As with any interest group, being on a trail run mailing list is a lot like checking in at the Hotel California. "You can check-out any time you like, but you can never leave." I received stacks of trail run registrations, newsletters and emails—not necessarily a bad thing. After only my second trail run among an endless list of road races, I experienced resurgence in my otherwise directionless running life. As time went on, I'd credit the grueling nature of trail running with improving my road race finishing times, as well as a key factor that enabled me to achieve previously unthinkable accomplishments in the sport that was my passion. Years later I looked back on those trail runs as some of my fondest running memories.

CHAPTER SIXTEEN

JOINING THE HALF-CENTENARIAN CLUB

I celebrated membership into the half-centenarian club along the Delaware Canal in Bucks County, PA, on a sunny July day in 2004. The towpath, parallel to the canal, was completed in 1832 to transport coal and other goods from Easton to Bristol, PA, but had been restored over the years to an eclectic trail shared by hikers, runners, cyclists, artists and naturalists who enjoy miles of pristine scenery. I discovered the Upper Delaware region when my kids were young and we'd explore for places to fish, canoe and camp. When they grew up, I'd play hooky from work and ride to the canal to spend the day running, fishing or just enjoying the outdoors. I couldn't think of a better way to spend my fiftieth birthday than to take a long run in one of the most scenic areas in the Mid-Atlantic States.

I set out for a run with no destination in mind, only to enjoy the rustic trail set between a lazy canal dotted with lily pads and frogs, and a mighty river full of bass, shad and muskie. I was content to run until my body said enough, which I estimated would be roughly thirteen miles. About an hour into the run, I realized the running junkie I had become. With sweat dripping down my face in the eighty-five degree heat on a day off, a voice inside my head repeated, *This is great!* over and over. The voice belonged to me. I'd run 30K five days earlier and I couldn't get enough.

Somewhere in the midst of the run, the dilemma I had struggled with seeped back into consciousness. The frustration I'd experienced trying to funnel the energy I invested into running to a medium that would benefit others intensified. I'd always found clairvoyance at its peak when I was immersed in sweat, and made an attempt to draw on that clarity to translate my passion into a message that would resonate and inspire others. I was determined not to give up until I succeeded, the same way I wouldn't give up at the twenty-mile mark of a marathon. The only way I knew to prevail was to plow through the barrier of uncertainty and persevere until the message emerged.

An interview I'd heard years earlier with a female author whose name I couldn't remember came to mind. She had shared a lesson her father passed down to her—that an individual could be the only bible another person may ever read. She went on to explain that a person's message could influence another's life without the perpetrator ever knowing. I found the concept fascinating and profound, and then wondered why the interview came to mind just as I was seeking guidance.

My quest became a challenge to transform my chronicles into a narrative that would motivate people to seek their passion, regardless if it was running, learning a craft, getting a degree or mastering a trade. I'd set out to find purpose in running, and now believed I was getting closer to the answer. I realized I'd been looking in the wrong places for a solution that was right in front of me. I was searching for that elusive meaning of life, and only needed to look within, find my voice and compose my message. As I approached the parking lot in Lumberville, I looked upward in thanksgiving for a glimpse at the solution to my quandary, and prayed for the courage to follow through.

CHAPTER SEVENTEEN

THE PLAN

If running a second marathon twenty years after my first was an epiphany, then attempting to qualify for the Boston Marathon during my fiftieth year on the planet was sheer genius. The idea of running Boston formulated in my head in early 2004, after rehabilitating my knee led to resurgence in my running.

The Boston Marathon is the most prestigious race in the world. A feature that lures athletes to the race is that a runner must qualify for the privilege of running the storied course. The qualifying times are based on gender and age. For example, in 2004 qualifying times began at 3:10:00 for males and 3:40:00 for females between the ages eighteen and thirty-four. The maximum qualifying time was 5:00:00 for males and 5:30:00 for females over eighty years old. The qualifying time for males in my age group, fifty to fifty-four was 3:35:00.

Running 26.2 miles may seem extraordinary to the general population, but it is not that unusual to athletes within the running community. Qualifying for a marathon in 3:35:00 at the age of fifty might seem incredible to the average layperson; however 3,058 men between the ages of fifty and fifty-nine finished Boston in 2011. Consider that Norm Green, Jr. ran the distance in an astonishing 2:27:42 at the youthful age of fifty-five, and 3:35:00 seems pedestrian. Whenever I needed an injection of humility, I would check race results online and count the number of runners in the sixty to sixty-nine age group who finished before me. There was no better remedy to keep from getting a big head.

I researched strategies to cut twenty minutes from the best finishing time I'd run since reincarnating my marathon career in 2001, which was 3:53:47 on Ocean Drive. I figured I could have finished closer to 3:40:00 had I not stopped for bio-breaks and to stretch cramped calve muscles, which gave me a slight psychological lift. However, I would also have to match a pace I had run twenty-three years earlier when I ran a 3:34:39 at twenty-seven years old.

I evaluated every conceivable angle to slash a few minutes here, a couple of minutes there. I posted requests on running forums for strategies to improve my time, and the response was overwhelming from the passionate cult I'd been drawn into. The advice ranged from boneheaded to simply profound, like "Why not shed a few pounds?" Several runners advised training at a faster pace, while others took time to share specific training regimens. I adopted advice that made the most sense to me and developed a program that included running hills and speed training, core-strengthening exercises and dropping weight. I pulled out all the stops—even gave up smoking an occasional cigar and, embarrassingly, switched my staple from Yuengling to Yuengling Light. I would make up for it and drink a Guinness every day for a month if I qualified.

I strategically selected the Steamtown Marathon in Scranton, Pennsylvania, to take advantage of the fast course with a 955-foot net elevation drop, which would hopefully cut another few minutes from my time. Based on the research I'd done, I would need to get my act together and begin serious training in July to prepare for Steamtown in October.

. . .

Training to complete a marathon in a specific time was completely different from training to simply finish. I began running intervals—high intensity bursts of speed alternated with recovery, usually a slow jog— and found a trail behind the Fox Chase Farm with killer hills that became routine training ground. The farm was across the road from the trailhead where I'd take long runs on the weekend, and I would add anywhere from two to eight miles of hills at the end of a workout. Hills can be punishing if you let them intimidate you, but I learned to make the hills my friend. Consequently, after weeks of tackling hills I began to look forward to them and they became effortless. I shed weight and my endurance increased. I began taking weekday mid-range runs of eight to ten miles, something I'd normally done only on weekends.

I couldn't remember exactly when it occurred, but one day I noticed a profound physical difference—I felt lighter and stronger. I was out for a run and suddenly found a kick in my stride that hadn't existed before. It was a subtle feeling that I didn't want to lose, so I devoted myself to the routine I had created.

For the first time ever, I timed myself during training runs. I never owned a runner's watch, actually didn't own a watch that worked, but the radio for my headset had a digital clock. By early August, I was surprised to run a sub-eight-minute mile on the seventh mile of a training run on the hills. It was an incredibly clean and healthy feeling. I registered for the ten-mile Captain Bill's Beach Run in Sea Isle City, New Jersey, for the second consecutive year, only this time I'd run on two good knees. It would be the first test to measure progress in my quest to qualify for Boston.

Captain Bill's was the last race I'd run before knee surgery the previous year, and I was determined to exorcise the demon that haunted me for ten miles along the water's edge. The race would serve as preparation for the Philadelphia Distance Run in September. I had planned to hook up with Ed before the race, but the starting line was a mass of bodies on a promenade narrow enough to spit across from one side to the other, which made the rendezvous unlikely.

I bumped into Jimmy's buddy Shawn and we lined up together for the starting gun. Shawn was a natural athlete, college soccer star and always in terrific condition, but he'd been out drinking until five in the morning. When we reached the end of the promenade and ran out onto the beach, Shawn said, "Hey Mr. B, I swear to God, I'll never drink the night before a race again."

"Yeah, Shawn, I know. We'll be running along the beach this time next year and you'll be telling me the same bullshit."

"No, Mr. B, I swear."

This went on for the first five miles until I couldn't take it any longer and I finally said, "Shawn, drinking is a lame excuse for lousy performance for anyone under thirty."

Shawn eventually recovered, and we rode the momentum of the thoroughbreds in the front of the field. I held back so I wouldn't burn out early on the slow sandy course, then found a rhythm around mile four and ran sub-eight-minute miles through mid-race, a pace I'd been unable to maintain since before knee surgery. I kept anticipating I'd fizzle; instead I felt stronger by the mile. At the eight-mile mark, my juices were flowing and at mile nine I decided to lay everything I had on the beach. When I saw the finish line I tore off my shirt and struck a near-sprint. There was no way of knowing how fast I ran the final mile, but I felt it was my strongest. I crossed the finish line at 1:17:12. Captain Bill's Beach Run gave me confidence that I had a shot to qualify for Boston.

I milled around after the race drinking water and eating fruit before I finally found Ed. We headed to Jimmy's shore house for a hot shower and some cold beers, the perfect remedy after running a beautiful ten-miler by the sea. Hanging out with the younger guys brought back memories of lost summers at the shore when we would close the bars, then watch the sunrise on the beach with a six-pack and a bottle of wine. But I didn't envy the hangover that awaited the boys Sunday morning. I was happy that I'd graduated to a lifestyle with rewards that included waking up clear-headed in a clean, comfortable bed with my honey by my side.

On my way out the door, I said to Jimmy, "Tell Shawn to train harder for next year and maybe I'd let him beat the old man." Jimmy and his friends laughed.

Walking to our cars, Ed asked, "Are you going to run the Halfwit next weekend?"

I had completely forgotten about the half-marathon, and said, "Are you?"

"I'm already signed up."

"Then I'm in. I'll talk to you during the week."

. . .

The Halfwit would be another race I'd gauge my progress to qualify at Steamtown in November. I was in the best physical condition I'd been in decades and felt I could shave time from my best half-marathon, until I realized the night before the race that it was a 13.1-mile trail run. Oh shit!

The Halfwit was an excruciating run, up and down mountains, including one climb appropriately named "150 Steps to Hell." I was astonished to run seven miles into a forest and find an old stone stairway climbing straight up the side of a mountain, with six-foot-high thorn bushes covering the top. Fortunately, by the time I reached the bushes I was too numb to care. Nevertheless, the climb was worth every ounce of sweat and pain because the water station at mile nine was stocked with cold beer. Not to take anything away from the benevolent guys and gals who set up the beer table in Manayunk and serve Yuengling at mile twenty-one of the Philly Marathon, but there wasn't a road anywhere in sight at the Halfwit, only trees, boulders and hills. I'd never seen a volunteer staff accomplish such a feat, but endorsed it as a requirement for all races.

After the race, the usual nicked, cut and bruised bodies filled the pavilion. I was discouraged when I saw 2:15:00 on the clock at the finish line. Then I considered I'd just navigated mountains, streams, mud, rocks, downed trees and "150 Steps to Hell," and felt somewhat less defeated. Always searching for an upside, I conceded to Ed that I never would have gone out alone and run 13.1 miles up and down mountains at such a pace. In retrospect, the Halfwit was an excellent training run for Steamtown.

The next day Joanne and I left for vacation in Ocean City, New Jersey. The boys were all working and Colleen would drive down with her friends later in the day. After we arrived and unpacked, I peddled to the Sixth Street track to run a few miles, already forgetting the pounding my body took less than twenty-four hours earlier. I ran 10K the following day, and by midweek I was running fifteen miles on the beach. It became increasingly obvious that I couldn't live without running. I understood Dr. Sheehan's philosophy regarding fitness: "But then my fitness program was never a fitness program. It was a campaign, a revolution, a conversion. I was determined to find myself. And, in the process, found my body and the soul that went with it."

Seven weeks remained until the qualifying race at Steamtown, and only five weeks of intense training. I'd planned to taper the two weeks preceding the marathon to allow my body time to recover for the race.

Through no intentions of my own, 2004 shaped up as the most prolific running year of my life. Without giving it a thought, I'd entered eight races—a 10K, two 20Ks, two 10-milers, two half-marathons and a 30K trail run—all before I got to Steamtown. I'd doubled the number of races I'd enter in a typical year, and all within twelve months after knee surgery.

CHAPTER EIGHTEEN

QUEST TO QUALIFY

My plan for the final two months leading to Steamtown included a seventeen, an eighteen and a nineteen-mile training run on three consecutive weekends. The longest run would be a twenty-miler at the Philadelphia Distance Run, where I'd continue after I crossed the finish line of the half-marathon out onto West River Drive for an additional seven miles.

The last Saturday in August, I drove to Pennypack Park for the seventeen-miler. I planned to start with a five-mile tract, followed by a seven-mile route through the steepest hills on the trail, before finishing with a double loop around Fox Chase Farm. I felt strong the first twelve miles in the oppressive ninety-degree heat, but suffered the final five miles. Perspiration flowed from every pore of my body as fast as I hydrated, and energy bars seemed ineffective. Considering the weather conditions, I was pleased to manage just over eight-minute miles. I knew the October climate in the mountains of northeast Pennsylvania, combined with adrenalin rush from the cheering crowd, would be in my favor at Steamtown. The momentum of the other runners and their camaraderie would be added advantages.

The next day both of my knees swelled. I didn't run Sunday or Monday, my first break from running on consecutive days in a long time. I had reservations about a layoff too close to the marathon, and didn't want to blow it after all the work I'd done getting into the best condition since high school football camp, maybe even my life. At the same time, I was leery of making the mistake I'd made when I beat my body to a pulp training for the 2001 Philly Marathon and was injured before I lined up for the starting gun.

I was tempted to take another day off on Tuesday, but nearly half a week seemed too long. It was an unusually hectic day at work and I didn't return home until after six o'clock. Joanne was still at work, so I changed into my running gear as soon as I walked through the door and hit the Tookany Creek trail. I started out slow to test the knee, which was still a little sore. By the time I got to the middle school track, I could feel the day's stress ooze from my body. Within fifteen minutes I forgot about the temptation I'd had to take another day off and was thankful I decided to end the brief hiatus.

I warmed-up running around the quarter-mile track, and then ripped off some 400-meter and 800-meter laps at a steady pace. Before I started the training program I didn't even know the distance of 400 or 800 meters. The only speed work I had ever done was running fartleks—a training method developed by a Swedish cross-country coach that alternates running intensity during a long, continuous workout. Fartleks differ from intervals, for the most part, because they can be run at random distances and paces, a feature that fit my personality. I averaged a sub-eight-minute-mile pace, faster than I needed to qualify. The pace was significant because I glided effortlessly, rather than labor to hit the mark. When I was finished the speed work I ran repetitions up the hills, and then another mile around the track before heading home through the park. On my return down the trail I knocked two minutes from the thirteen-minutes it normally took to cover the distance—a motivating conclusion to the seventy-five minute run.

The weather Saturday morning was spectacular for running, in complete contrast from the conditions when I'd run the seventeen-miler a week earlier. The sun was blinding, but the temperature was in the low eighties without a trace of humidity. Less than two miles into the run I bumped into Ed. We struck a comfortable pace while we passed the time talking. Ed finished his run at mile ten and I headed back out for another five miles into Pennypack, then crossed Pine Road into Fox Chase Farm to further test my endurance. After the beating my body had taken the previous week, I didn't plan to run the hills behind the farm again before the race, but continued since I felt fresh and ran harder than I had the previous fifteen miles. The culmination of all the training and the two-day rest earlier in the week was the only explanation I could figure for my high energy level.

I recalled a fellow runner's advice suggesting that I run my hardest during the final miles of a training session, and found myself surprisingly strong attacking the hills. I listened to the gentle thumping of my heartbeat in perfect harmony with the rhythm of my breath as I inhaled, then exhaled— a symphony created by a well-conditioned body in motion. As I closed in on the final miles of the eighteen-mile run, the symphony was overtaken by Jim Morrison's anthem, "Break on Through to the Other Side," playing over and over in my head. When I finished I leaned down and put my hands on my knees and watched the sweat drip onto my running shoes and the grassy trail. After the strongest long-run in memory, I raised my head and looked out over the pasture where the livestock were my only witnesses. I was at peace and my confidence grew to a level I hadn't felt since I began the training program—I was at ease in body and spirit.

. . .

The effects of the long training program took its toll, and the following weekend I had to force myself through the first half of a laborious nineteen-mile run. I ran from a sense of duty, rather than the sense of joy I experienced a week earlier. I knew from experience neither to get too high nor too low during training, just to persevere and do the work— not always an easy thing to do when the task is a nineteen-mile run. Still, I knew at some point the juices would begin to flow and endorphins would emit to ease my struggle. I finished the run exhausted, but a wholesome exhaustion, and I woke Sunday morning reassured that struggling through the run would pay off well after I crossed the finish line in Scranton.

. . .

I was out of town at a conference in Austin, Texas, the week of the Distance Run and planned only a few short maintenance runs. After I checked in at the Royal Crown Hotel on Monday afternoon, I asked the receptionist the usual question, "Where is a good place to run around here?" She gave me that odd look I'd grown accustomed to and pointed down the road toward a trail she referred to as Town Lake.

The multitude of runners and cyclists on the Town Lake trail, and scullers rowing on the Colorado River, reminded me of Kelly Drive. Soccer players practiced on ball fields adjacent to the trail. The energy radiating from all the young athletes indicated I was in a college town. I ran fartleks on a 10.1-mile loop in sweltering, mid-ninety degree Texas heat, but felt great. I returned to the hotel drenched, but invigorated.

Sweat streamed from my body when I ran into some people from the conference on their way to dinner. They invited me to join them and I said I'd catch up with them later, though I had no such intention. I went up to my room, took a cool shower and relaxed, then walked to a TexMex restaurant and wound up joining a half dozen folks I recognized. After dinner we walked down Sixth Street to digest our burritos and salsa, when we heard our names shouted from inside a funky little blues bar. Without breaking stride we meandered in and joined the well-lubricated crew for beers.

A blues band wailed as we made our way across the bar. A heavyset, middle-aged guy played harmonica and a tall, lanky drummer was in the background. A young lady on bass had a set of steel vocal cords that reminded me of Janice Joplin. But the lead guitarist grabbed my attention. He was an older guy with a cowboy hat down to the tip of his nose and an eternal cigarette dangling from his lips. He appeared the quintessential bar musician, a lifer, committed to his craft and so completely in tune with the rhythm, that he *was* the music. He jumped up and down, though the tips of his cowboy boots barely left the floor, picked the strings with his teeth like Jimi Hendrix, played it behind his head, and when he took off solo the other band members followed his lead.

I stood at the bar sipping a cold beer, watching the guitarist, and contemplated the similarities between a lifer lead guitarist lost in a solo and a runner absorbed in the zone. It seemed to me that anyone who reached such a state of being, whether a musician, runner, carpenter, or writer, transcended their vocation, or avocation, to a higher level of consciousness and fulfillment. The guitar player was in a zone. He had that same look in his eye that I saw in the old-timer at sixty-eight-hundred feet on Mount Rainier the week of 9-11, and in the eyes of the two seasoned bikers who rode one thousand miles from Orange County, California to Washington State. It was the unmistakable glimmer I saw in the eyes of bikers I'd pass on weekends on River Road in Bucks County. I knew that look because I'd seen it in the eyes of so many runners after they crossed the finish line at long distance races.

Martha Graham, a pioneer of modern dance, observed, "No artist is ahead of his time. He is his time; it is just that others are behind the times." In the middle of a wailing solo the guitar player was, without a doubt, in his time. There was no difference between the state of mind he was in playing his guitar and the peaceful place I'd visit in the midst of a three-hour run.

. . .

The Brennan household was in mayhem the week before the Distance Run. Joanne was preparing for Gina's bridal shower, Jay's future bride. It was no normal shower, but an elegant tea. There was a twenty-five-by-thirty-foot tent to be erected in the backyard, and tables and seating for over fifty guests. Scores of tea cups, saucers and settings were stacked on every table and square inch of counter space. Everything was homemade, from dainty tea sandwiches to pastries. I had no concept of what a tea was until the shower, but I'd learned it is the antithesis of a tailgate party.

That same week, work had been more hectic than usual, and I did my best to get ready for the longest run on the training program. The Distance Run would be the foundation for the twenty-miler, and a reality check of whether my expectations to qualify for Boston were realistic.

After a restless night's sleep I woke up Sunday morning and saw the sun for the first time in four days. I ducked my head out the back door to a cool and breezy morning—near perfect running conditions. I ate oatmeal sprinkled with wheat germ and raisins then packed my gear, grabbed a coffee, Gatorade and Cliff Bar, kissed Joanne on the forehead and drove downtown with U2 vibrating against the Jeep windows.

Considering I had only a few hours sleep, I was functioning reasonably well. I merged onto the Vine Street Expressway, exited at Ben Franklin Parkway and found a parking space at Sixteenth and Callowhill Streets. After I changed into my running gear, I started a slow jog toward City Hall. The vibration of blaring music echoed off the tall buildings as I nudged my way to a starting spot among seven thousand runners.

Pace groups are designated with signs to avoid logjams of runners at the start of large races. Runners who plan to run a six-minute mile pace line up at the six-minute mile sign, and each successive pace group follows suit. It took me years to figure out that if you're planning to run an eight-minute mile pace, don't line up with the eight-minute mile pace group unless you wanted to spend the first few miles dodging runners with unrealistic expectations. Invariably, some overzealous novices line up at a pace they'd have a hard time maintaining if they were cycling. After years of subjecting myself to such aggravation, I got smart and joined the back of the six-minute mile pace group, closed my eyes, relaxed and said a prayer.

It took only a few minutes after the starting gun sounded to figure out it was going to be a good race. The mass of runners proceeded east on Market Street toward the Delaware River, then turned south before returning west on South Street through town. The crowd was dense, and I worked to settle into a rhythm using the pace group's energy and momentum to my advantage. I pushed a pace slightly faster than I would normally run and looked ahead for runners to pick off.

After passing through downtown, the course turned onto the Ben Franklin Parkway toward the Art Museum then veered left for the most scenic stretch of the race—The River Drives. As I headed out West River Drive I looked over my right shoulder at Boathouse Row, The Water Works, Art Museum and Philadelphia skyline, a metropolitan panorama I contended was as spectacular as any in the nation in debates with out-of-towners. At the end of West River Drive I followed the runners across the Falls Bridge and turned right onto Kelly Drive. I winked at the bronze sculpture of John Kelly, the three-time Olympic gold medalist oarsman, as I ran by the grandstands, and then passed under the rock tunnel leading to the Victorian structures of Boathouse Row. The race's only hill behind the Art Museum led to the final mile on the Parkway and around Logan Circle before ending just before City Hall.

I ran as hard as I could across the finish line at 1:40:06, placing in the top twenty percent of both the field and my age group, averaging 7:38 per mile, well under what I needed to qualify for Boston. I dropped my chip into a box and headed back out the parkway and onto West River Drive for the additional seven miles to cap off the final long run on the training program. I backed off to an 8:00-minute pace for the final miles, but felt strong with energy to spare. My confidence soared—I was convinced I would qualify for Boston.

. . .

Only three weeks remained before I would line up for the Steamtown Marathon. The only long runs remaining on the program were a 13-miler and a one-hour run. I would also do some 400-meter and 800-meter intervals at three-quarter speed to maintain a healthy stride. My confidence was so high I started to believe I could finish Boston in under 3:30:00.

Jay's bachelor party was planned for the weekend before Steamtown. There was nothing in the training manual about three days of partying with a bunch of guys twenty years my junior so close to the marathon, so I had to rely on my own instincts. Four o'clock Friday afternoon I became antsy sitting in the Pentagon at a meeting with a four-star general, more eager to join my boys to celebrate the final days Jay would spend as a single man than conversing with a man who controlled hundreds of billions of dollars of the Army's budget. My mind kept creeping back to the Amtrak ticket for the six o'clock train to Philly that was inside my suit jacket pocket.

The briefing had ended, but an executive from my Washington headquarters insisted on making small talk with the general and lobbying for more work. The clock ticked toward four-thirty and I began making escape plans. As my mind raced, I wondered how the hell I went from climbing through ships' bilges as an apprentice welder twenty-some years earlier to a meeting in the Pentagon with a military powerbroker. I recalled the promotion to foreman at twenty-five, years in night school to earn a degree, a stint as an industry analyst, and then finally becoming the manager of an organization full of engineers, financial analysts and economists. That was the road that led from the Vegetable Aisle to the Pentagon; from Dumb-Dumb to Sir—and I hated being called Sir. I hated it so much that I would sometimes correct people and yell, "Jim. My name is Jim!" People would tell me that standing in the five-sided building in Virginia where the nation conducted plans to preserve the peace was an achievement, but I wanted out.

As soon as the meeting concluded, I hopped a ride to the Metro and headed for Union Station to catch the six o'clock Acela back to Philly. Uncharacteristic for Friday afternoon rush hour in DC, everything went like clockwork and I arrived at the Thirtieth Street Station in Philly at seven-thirty, jumped into Joanne's Mustang and sped west on the Schuylkill Expressway. I pulled into the driveway and ran into the house a little past eight o'clock, showered, ate dinner, grabbed my golf clubs and a case of beer, kissed Joanne goodbye and ran out the back door.

Adrenalin replaced exhaustion when I emerged from the tunnel on the Northeast Extension of the Pennsylvania Turnpike and crossed the bridge over the Lehigh River just south of Lehighton. I expected the long day would finally come to an end when I pulled into the driveway of the cabin the boys had rented in Bartonsville, Pennsylvania, around midnight. Instead, when I turned off the engine I heard the sound of loud, rowdy voices bellowing through the thick log walls and knew it was only beginning. I opened the door and walked into the middle of a lively and passionate game of Texas Hold 'em and was immediately handed a cold beer and dealt a hand at a makeshift poker table. The boys were feeling no pain and we played cards through the night. I needed to get some rest before the golf outing that would begin in only a few hours and crawled into a cot in the loft sometime before daybreak. I fell asleep thinking about a revolutionary marathon-training program that combined drinking and sleep deprivation with fartleks and hill sprints.

Saturday was a payback for all of the years I bragged about never getting sick. It had rained through the night and the golf course was waterlogged. Some fairways were completely submerged and I was soaked from the moment we teed off on the first hole, and by the third hole I thought I'd grown gills. The rain stopped when we reached the fifth hole, but much of the course remained under water. The weather didn't dampen the boys' spirits and beer flowed from the back of Dan and Jim's golf cart, whenever they weren't chasing deer through the woods. Their boisterous laughter was distracting enough to keep my mind from a sore throat that had taken hold. Considering the boys only turned-over one golf cart, we concluded the outing a success. Dan gave me strict instructions to buy cough medicine and throat lozenges for the ride home to Philly after dinner.

Sunday morning I was greeted by the groggy feeling that follows a sound and restful sleep. I rose from bed like a stumbling drunk after a week-long bender, staggered to the kitchen and fumbled to make a pot of coffee while I considered breakfast. Though I was fighting a cold, I rejected the notion of abandoning the long run. At halftime of the Eagles game, I changed into my running gear and made my way out the back door and walked to Tookany Creek before breaking into a slow jog. The bright sun shone in my face and my spirits were lifted by a run I had forced upon myself.

The beginning of the week I took short-mileage runs and when I returned from work Thursday, I headed out for the last run before the race. I felt strong, fresh and confident, and thought the cold might have helped because I had slept more than usual. Thursday night I posted a message in a marathon forum asking for last minute advice, and Friday there were eleven responses. There was no specific advice I hadn't heard or read elsewhere, but I sensed a passion that dripped from the words of my fellow marathoners—*Go out slow, find your pace group, hydrate, stay calm early, enjoy the ride.* I was so psyched I had to keep myself in check, and it was only Friday night.

I woke well-rested Saturday morning and ate like a caveman the entire day, devouring protein, carbohydrates and potassium found in oatmeal, PowerBars, figs and pasta and washed it all down with Gatorade. If I cramped up or bonked during the race it wasn't going to be from poor nutrition.

After breakfast, I sat in front of the keyboard and attempted to describe my feelings the day before the race. The chronicle I'd begun while training for the 2001 Philly Marathon had continued for another three years, and now, the day before the most important race in my life, I was incapable of translating my feelings into words. The writer's block was frustrating because I knew I would experience absolute clarity during the marathon the following day. It was even more perplexing because most times that clarity would dissipate before I got home later in the day. Nevertheless, I persevered and wrote about the point somewhere between the halfway mark and the finish line when my *work* would make perfect sense. I anticipated tranquility within the 26.2 miles, a tranquility I was unable to find by any other means. And I would be there in less than twenty-four hours.

I planned to leave a note for Joanne with instructions for her to open it Sunday morning at the time I estimated to be at the midway point of the marathon. It was unlikely that words would help a non-runner feel the emotion of running 26.2 miles, but I was determined to give it my best shot. I dug into the deepest emotions I'd experienced during long training runs and previous marathons and wrote them down. When I could do no more, I stuffed the letter in an envelope and left it with instructions to open at nine-forty-five Sunday morning, when I hoped to be into the fourteenth mile. The note read:

Honey,

I'm past the halfway point of the marathon and have paid the dues to enter a zone so indescribably peaceful I'm reminded of why I do this. At this moment, life makes perfect sense and I am keenly appreciative of everything God has given me, especially you, the kids, our families, our health.

I never want to leave this zone, but soon I will pass the twenty-mile mark and confront the miles on the other side. You see, marathoners believe that the twenty-mile mark is the halfway point of the marathon, that the final six miles require as much effort and more pain as the previous twenty. I will test myself those final six miles to see what I'm made of, for the marathon is, "Twenty miles of hope, and six miles of truth." When I cross the finish line it will all have been worth it, and somehow I know I'll be back doing it again.

Think of me at 11:30, when I'll be finished my work, hugging Colleen with my sweaty body and thanking God for you and all my blessings.

Love,
Your Man

I sealed the envelop and smiled as I imagined Joanne shaking her head with a perplexed expression on her face when she read the note Sunday morning, and then I laughed out loud. Jo and I were living proof that opposites attract. She loved oldies, and I couldn't blast Pearl Jam and Green Day loud enough; she'd watch old black and white movies, while my inclination leaned toward Pulp Fiction and the Big Lebowski; Jo didn't like the taste of alcohol and I couldn't get enough Guinness in me. Joanne was artsy and I was a jock, though I unearthed an inclination toward the arts as I aged. But we shared the same core principles— our family came before everything else. It was a proven formula that strengthened our bond for more than thirty years.

. . .

Late Saturday afternoon I kissed Joanne goodbye and drove to Scranton where I'd meet Shawn and Paul, two of Jimmy's closest friends, later in the evening. Steamtown would be Shawn's first marathon. Colleen was attending the University of Scranton and volunteered to pick up our bib numbers and chips for the race, so I stopped at her apartment and wound up talking and laughing with her and her girlfriends for over an hour. Col's bluntness and sense of humor always made me laugh. When she was growing up, she had affectionate nicknames for me like Fat Boy and Bald Spot. One memorable line she screamed at me when all of her friends were over the house one night was, "Why can't I have a normal father like everyone else?" I would chuckle at the thought of that line for years afterward. There was no better way to relax before the biggest race of my life than hanging out with a bunch of college girls. I bid Col and her friends farewell around eleven and made the short drive south to Wilkes-Barre to hook up with the boys.

Shawn and Paul arrived from the other direction as I pulled into the dreary parking lot at the Wilkes-Barre Days Inn. We grabbed our gear, checked into the hotel and went to a small room with two beds, but not the cot I had reserved. It was just as well because watching the two lugs, both former college athletes, crammed into a queen-size bed was hysterical. I made one last call to the front desk for a five-fifteen wake-up, set my cell phone alarm as backup, and turned the light out around midnight. Shawn broke Paul's balls until we all fell asleep and picked-up the second we woke five hours later. I lay in bed and laughed harder than I had since I was their age.

CHAPTER NINETEEN

STEAMTOWN

When the alarm went off Sunday morning, it seemed as though we'd just turned out the light, not exactly the amount of sleep recommended for the night prior to a marathon—especially a race with so much at stake. But rather than wake up alone in an empty room and cringe at the prospect of a day full of meetings and PowerPoint presentations as I had for so many years on business trips, I woke to the sound of two guys in their mid-twenties cursing and exchanging insults. There was no better way to begin the day I would make my first attempt to qualify for Boston than in the presence of two characters that made me feel twenty years younger. Paul planned to meet us at mile twenty-one and run to the finish line with Shawn. We corroborated plans, threw a few parting insults at Paul and hugged farewell.

Shawn and I drove to Scranton and boarded a bus before daybreak. The bus made its way along winding mountain roads and through small towns while a buzz hovered inside as the runners tried to restrain the adrenalin rush until the starting gun. Countless energy bars, gels and bottles of Gatorade were consumed before arriving in Forest City, Pennsylvania, where the race would begin.

Most people would be challenged to find Forest City on a map. Those who recognize the small mountain hamlet are likely people who venture twenty-three miles northeast of Scranton to fish, hunt or pick apples, rather than to line up for a marathon. It is a peaceful setting to embark on a torturous journey. When the bus pulled up to Forest City High School a group of students wearing ear-to-ear smiles cheered the runners and handed out ribbons and water bottles. Dawn had barely lifted and the morning already had the ingredients for a perfect marathon day: energy, sun, temperature in the low fifties and not a trace of humidity.

We walked into a gym strewn with runners and found a spot to chill. Runners slept on the floor while others meditated. Some exchanged strategies on how they would retrace on foot the 26.2 mile-route the bus had driven them. Still others carried on as if it were a party. I'd always found a marathon a cross between a challenge and a happening; a recital and a folk festival. Except for the top few percent competing to place for a prize, most run to test their own physical endurance. Serious runners always look for that elusive personal record, or PR, but most are happy to go home with a medal, T-shirt and the satisfaction of knowing they are among a minority of inhabitants on the planet who can run 26.2 miles. It is a race for the first hundred or so runners—it is a run for the rest.

. . .

The clock read seven-fifteen and I began to stretch. A voice came over the loud speaker and announced teams of fathers, sons, mothers, daughters and husbands and wives among the field of fourteen hundred runners. At seven-thirty I took my final bio-break, stretched some more and walked outside to the starting line. Locals dressed in Civil War garb stood next to a cannon in the middle of a field adjacent to the school. At the conclusion of the *Star Spangled Banner* the Grand Marshal wished the runners a safe journey and sent off the wheelchair athletes. Anxious runners stretched and jogged in place waiting for those familiar words. A few minutes passed before the proclamation, "On your mark, get set." Suddenly the mountaintop shook and smoke rose out of the barrel of the cannon. We were off.

Forest City residents were out in force on porches, lining front lawns and on sidewalks cheering the runners. A news helicopter flew over-head. The race's billing as a top Boston qualifier lived up to its repu-tation in the first seven miles, which were mostly downhill. Downhill distance running is counterintuitive and can be a double-edged sword. The natural tendency to accelerate the pace early in the race comes with the risk of depleting glycogen which can cause leg cramps as a runner progresses into the later stages. Consequently, it is wise to exercise meas-ured caution in the early miles.

Unlike many of the larger races, there were no digital clocks at the mile markers before the halfway point. I bothered a runner for a split (runners' terminology for the time it takes to complete specific distances) at mile five and calculated that I was averaging a 7:40-mile pace, completely blowing my strategy to run an 8:15-mile pace in the early miles. I tried to hold back, but found it too difficult. All of the speed work and hill training I'd done, combined with the downhill course made running seem effortless.

The course leveled off after mile eight and I clocked 1:39 at the halfway point, faster than I had in the Distance Run three weeks earlier, but I still had 13.1 miles to go. I asked a young woman runner for a split at mile fourteen and was still running a 7:45-mile pace. Feeling surprisingly strong with no sign of fatigue, my thoughts switched to Joanne. It was about the time she would open the note I had left for her in which I'd struggled to express the indescribable, but I nailed it. I was in that exceedingly peaceful state of mind, and contented as I ran through the fall mountain foliage surrounded by thousands of my fellow-runners. I was at that place I described in my message to her, "Where life makes perfect sense."

Approaching mile fifteen, the course eased onto a section of "Rails to Trails" that follows the Lackawanna River for about two miles. The sound of the water rambling over rocks along the riverbed refreshed my mind, and I settled into an energized rhythm. Shortly after passing mile eighteen, loud music and a large crowd greeted the runners at the entrance of Mellow Park. Volunteers handed out drinks and fruit as fans screamed encouragement to runners making a loop around a track. Exiting the park with the sun shining in my face I crossed the bridge over the Lackawanna into Condella Park near mile marker nineteen. Only seven miles remained—a 10K plus one mile.

I arrived at the point of the marathon where training programs will get most runners to, but the most challenging part was still ahead. Training, by itself, doesn't prepare a runner for the final six miles, and I prayed for physical and mental strength to push through to the finish. I'd always believed that sticking it out through life's toughest challenges was psychological conditioning for the marathon, just as the twenty-mile training run was for the physical conditioning. The mental tenacity required to push through a grueling endurance race is garnered from handling adversity and persevering through long hours of work, sick children, broken down cars, bad teachers, sick pets, bad jobs, business travel, broken bones and lousy bosses. A training program can get you to mile twenty, but after beating your body into oblivion for hours, mental toughness gets you through those "Six miles of truth."

I was comfortable in my cadence when a young runner came up from behind and said, "There's still a lot of pain that lie ahead."

I turned, looked him in the eye and said, "Think only positive thoughts, man! Never, ever, let a negative thought formulate in your mind during the course of a marathon." I needed to get some positive energy flowing and shared the words for my own benefit as well as his. The distance is too long and too grueling, and once the seed of negativity is sown, there is risk it will find fertile soil and germinate; then it doesn't matter how many miles remain, you are doomed. If a negative thought begins to nudge its way into the mind, find a distraction. Begin talking to someone, even yourself. Start singing, sightseeing or praying. If you wear an iPod, blast the damn thing—U2, Red Hot Chili Peppers, Foo Fighters, The Killers . . . louder, louder! I'd always keep a one-decade rosary in my pocket during a marathon, knowing that during the course of three or four hours there would be time to say it at least once. I'd pray for my family, those less fortunate than I, for the other runners, or in the case of the last few miles I'd pray for perseverance. It became my way of finding strength at the moment the well was near empty.

Somewhere after mile twenty-one in Dickson City, I thought I was delusional when I heard my name faintly in the distance. Next thing I knew, Paul was running beside me with a bottle of Gatorade. Paul's contagious enthusiasm was a welcomed boost. He seemed amazed and remarked how great I looked so far into the race, which I found hard to believe. We talked for about a half-mile and I told him to find Shawn, who probably needed more help than me in his first attempt at 26.2. I took one more gulp of Gatorade, thanked him and we bid one another farewell.

A family handed out bottles of water to the runners at a table they set up outside their house at mile twenty-three. I grabbed a bottle, took a few sips and leaned down to place it on the curb when I was suddenly hobbled by a sharp pain that pierced through my right calf. I continued cautiously with a soft, deliberate stride using my entire foot—landing on my heels and pushing off on my toes—in an attempt to stretch the calf muscle without stopping. I was afraid if I stopped to stretch, it would be the first in a series of interruptions that I couldn't afford. Even though I was ahead of the pace I needed to maintain, I wasn't about to take any chances to jeopardize qualifying for Boston.

After hours of running through the mountains and small towns of rural Pennsylvania, the course transitioned to the urban setting of Dunmore, a small borough adjoining Scranton. It was familiar turf from my days at Marywood University, or I should say Andy Gavins' Irish Pub down the street. I had never passed Gavins' without stopping for a pint of Guinness, but knew I'd be back later in the day. Dunmore was a festival—music blasted and a raucous crowd lined the streets handing runners drinks and snacks while screaming encouragement to exhausted athletes who accepted any incentive thrown their way.

At the end of the street, before turning toward downtown Scranton, a group of kids in wheelchairs from the Saint Joseph's Center, which cares for children afflicted with an array of mental disabilities, were lined up around a curve. The children were the most uplifting sight I'd seen on the entire 26.2-mile course. Their smiling faces were a reminder of how truly blessed I was, and inspired me to push through to the finish line.

For all of the buildup about the 955-foot drop from start to finish, the course designer was either unable to find a way around the long uphill leading to downtown or was a masochist. The cramps spread to my other calf and the pain affected my ability to maintain any type of rhythm, so I hunkered down and prepared to battle my rebelling body the remainder of the way. I struggled to keep pace with a runner who gave me a 3:18 split at mile twenty-five. Under normal circumstances finishing under 3:30:00 would be a breeze, but now my condition was deteriorating with each step. The thought that qualifying was slipping away in the final mile infuriated me. I looked up the hill that crested at the top of Washington Avenue, thought about the kids from Saint Joseph's Center, and promised myself that regardless how paralyzing the cramps became, nothing would stop me from crossing the finish line in under 3:35:00.

My knees locked as I ascended the hill on stiffened legs, resembling the stride of a stickman. I hadn't experienced debilitating leg cramps in thirty-five years of running, until now. I bent down several times and dug my knuckles into my calf muscles and kneaded them like dough in a futile attempt to ease the pain. Spectators screamed at me to keep going as I struggled to the top of the hill. I respected their pleas and pressed on, assuring them I would never quit. As I inched over the peak of the hill I saw the finish line outside City Square. I squinted through blurry eyes to read the time on the clock, and then heard the announcer congratulate a runner for finishing with what sounded like a 3:30:00 finishing time, but I couldn't be sure. I had five minutes to run the last four blocks, a feat I'd been able to do in less than half that time since first grade, but was now a challenge.

The finish line was so vivid it was as though I could reach out and touch it. Delirious, my mind tried to convince my body to sprint the final few hundred yards down Washington Avenue, but my legs wouldn't cooperate. I kept moving my stiffened legs as fast as I could and felt as if I was in a dream, running through quicksand and going nowhere. Two blocks from the finish line I finally had a clear view of the clock clicking toward 3:30:00. I would not be denied.

One block from the finish line the familiar voice of a screaming young woman stood out among the thousands that came to cheer their loved ones. I looked over and saw Colleen and choked back tears. A volunteer ran out and asked if I needed help. Though grateful, I waved him away and told him I'd cross the finish line under my own power, even if I had to crawl.

The next sensation was the cushioning of a soft rubber mat that covered the finish line to protect sensors that picked up a signal from the computer chip tied to my shoe lace that recorded 3:31:25. The pain I had experienced minutes earlier limping that final mile down Washington Avenue disappeared when I realized I had qualified. I'd cut twenty-five minutes from the best time I had run since reviving my marathon career in 2001, and finished three minutes faster than I had run the 1981 Philadelphia Independence Marathon at the age of twenty-seven.

My calves felt as though rocks were implanted behind the shinbones. I was in agony and never felt so good at the same time. I limped to the end of the runner's chute and smiled when I saw my little girl. In a rare moment of indifference toward stench and sweat, Colleen ran over and without hesitation threw her arms around my neck and gave me the biggest hug ever.

I was cooling down and describing the race to Colleen and her girl-friends when a loud, enthusiastic and boisterous voice interrupted. "Hey, Mr. B." It was Shawn with an ear-to-ear smile after just completing his first marathon. Paul was close behind laughing, accustomed to the spectacle that Shawn created whenever he was excited about anything, which was just about every second of every day.

"Congratulations, Shawn. How do you feel?"

"Great!" he shouted as if I were two blocks away.

I smiled, thinking of my first marathon in 1981 when my father greeted me with a hug and cooler full of cold beer on Chestnut Street in downtown Philly. Colleen and her girlfriends from the university circled us listening to adrenalin-pumped stories when Shawn blurted out, "Who the F#!K put that hill in the last mile?"

Instinctively, I hauled back and punched him in the chest. His shoulders heaved forward and the girls gasped, as if to say, Why did you do that? which Colleen in fact said, "Dad, why did you do that?"

That question from my twenty-year-old daughter made me feel my age more than the twenty-six miles I'd just run, and I didn't have an answer. Finally, I stammered, "Watch your language, Shawn," a response that would have been adequate in the company of my wife, or mother, or an assembly of the Catholic Daughters back in the 1960s, but sounded lame, even to me, standing among a group of college students in 2004. The dozen sets of eyes staring at me, mostly those of young women, told me that I was a tad of touch.

Shawn laughed as if I'd just told a joke and said, "No problem, Mr. B," as enthusiastically as he dropped the F-bomb.

As the afternoon wore on, Colleen's girlfriends disappeared back to their dorms, and Shawn and Paul walked to their car for the ride home. Colleen helped me limp from City Square to my Jeep under an impossibly bright sun. She was juggling all the things that a college student handles, and I didn't want to hold her up, so I hugged my sweetheart goodbye on a street corning in downtown Scranton. She looked at me and said, "Hey, Dad. Guess what?"

"What?"

"You're going to Boston."

CHAPTER TWENTY

INTROSPECTION

The reason I run is a mystery, even to me. Running is imbedded so deep into my being that after forty years of pounding the pavement and trails I found myself running farther than ever as I aged, and enjoyed it more than in past decades. I passed previous milestones in my life wondering why friends always complained about blood pressure, cholesterol and triglycerides while I continued to enter half-marathons and marathons. I would say, "If it took me fifty years to qualify for the Boston Marathon, just think what I'll be able to do by the time I reach one hundred."

Scottish writer and poet Muriel Spark once said, "Be on the alert to recognize your prime at whatever time of your life it may occur." I was going to Boston for the first time at fifty, and felt I had yet to hit my prime.

· · ·

I'd experienced such euphoria after crossing the finish line at Steamtown, it was incomprehensible to imagine the feeling I would have running the storied course at Boston. The physical and psychological rewards of my qualifying race exceeded those of past marathons, where I had been satisfied to simply finish in less than four hours. The training program had become self-perpetuating and infiltrated other aspects of my life. I was upbeat and had boundless energy.

During the later stages of the training program, a mysterious thing happened. Once I noticed improvement, I looked forward to the workouts. I never thought the day would come when I'd enjoy running intervals and uphill sprints. The mile intervals became easier and the hills became my friend. Confidence permeated my psyche the same way perspiration flowed over every centimeter of my body during a long run. My confidence was so high by race day that nothing short of a defrocked Irish priest tackling me on the course would keep me from my goal, just like what to what happened to Brazilian marathoner Vanderlei Lima in the 2004 Olympic marathon. I recalled the disbelief in Lima's face that day, when the priest emerged from the crowd and knocked him off stride three miles from the finish line. The Brazilian wound up winning the bronze medal, a small consolation considering he was on pace to win gold.

Common sense suggested I should have taken a break from training, but I was tempted to run the Philadelphia Marathon in November. Many trainers and coaches advise allowing three to four months recovery before subjecting the body to the pounding of another marathon. I naively thought I could cut my recovery time in half if I trained moderately and lowered the long run to either eighteen-miles or two and one-half hours. My main concern was to remedy the paralyzing calf cramps that hobbled me the final miles of Steamtown. The weeks following the marathon I would jump out of bed at night screaming and limping around the bedroom like someone hit me in the calves with a Louisville Slugger. The cramps even forced me to swim to the side of the pool to avoid drowning when I swam with the Special Olympians on Friday nights. I scheduled an appointment with an orthopedic specialist who had once been the US Olympic Track & Field team doctor. He prescribed shoe inserts and recommended increasing my potassium intake before long races, but neither solution entirely eliminated the cramps.

As the end of October approached, I was revitalized and completed a thirteen-mile run effortlessly. I decided to wait and see how I felt after an eighteen-miler I had planned before I registered for Philly, but suffered a slight stress fracture in my right foot before it ever occurred. I felt like a hypocrite because I ignored the advice I'd given to other runners. "Listen to your body," I would say, "an injury is the body telling you to rest." Now *I* had a stress fracture, and likely from overuse.

I backed off from running forty miles per week and reverted to cycling and lifting light-weights. Three weeks before the race I tested the stress fracture with a short three-mile run on soft terrain and didn't experienced any pain. Then I came to my senses. A series of long training runs to prepare for a second marathon, six weeks after the best race I'd ever run, was an invitation for serious injury. I decided with my head rather than my heart for a change, and opted out of the Philly Marathon.

. . .

The twenty-eight-week stretch between Steamtown and the Boston Marathon in April 2005 was the longest gap I'd had between races in over a year. I'd been frantically scurrying on the hamster wheel for so long—jamming a marathon training program between work, paying bills and raising a family—that I'd never given much thought about where I'd been or where I was going. During the downtime, I became philosophical and introspective. I marveled that I'd managed to navigate through life and arrive at age fifty with a family that made me proud, a relatively successful career and my sanity somewhat intact. Yet sinister insecurities lurked below the surface that ate at the fragile sheathing of a perceived healthy existence, and it exposed glaring flaws.

The inadequacies I'd battled since my formative years would creep back unexpectedly and haunt me. I had buried the ghosts of Dumb-Dumb and shed the stigma of the Vegetable Aisle decades ago, yet, somehow during vulnerable emotional swings they'd seep into consciousness. Only now, decades and thousands of miles later, I knew I could seek refuge in the long run to dispel their hold. Running grounded me and eradicated the self-doubt.

When I began a welding apprenticeship at the shipyard after high school, former teachers and coaches were aghast when they learned of my profession. One priest I had confided in over the years said, "Well, you don't want to do that for the rest of your life," and suggested I look for another job. I must have been missing something, because I enjoyed my trade and took pride in working at the shipyard. I was promoted to foreman when I was in my mid-twenties, which I attributed to the same drive and perseverance required to run a marathon, rather than to intellectual prowess. I started taking management classes at night and when the credits began to accumulate I persisted the only way I knew how to earn my bachelor's degree—I plowed my way through to graduation. The

Cum Laude on my college diploma was more a testament to hardhead-edness and drive than to brains.

Years later I wondered what the warden of the Vegetable Aisle would have thought had she known I would one day brief four-star generals in the Pentagon and CEOs of multi-billion dollar international corpora-tions on the health of manufacturing industries. A close friend of mine had a succinct response for such ignorance. Bud and I were welders and foremen at the shipyard, until his career path steered south to the nation's capital. We would meet for a beer whenever I traveled to DC on business and rehash the good old days over a pint. Bud would get this wild look in his eye, then a huge grin would spread across his face and he'd laugh, "Not bad for goddamn welders, eh?" an eloquent response for all those righteous, narrow-minded people who'd judged me solely on superficies factors as a youth.

. . .

I'd attended countless management and leadership seminars, but distinctly recalled the first seminar as a young production supervisor at the shipyard in South Philadelphia. The instructor, like every instructor and management consultant I listened to thereafter, claimed to have the formula for success—the keys to the kingdom. The students sat in a circle, and near the conclusion of his dissertation he made a dramatic pause. Everyone leaned forward intently and he simply said, "Just Do It!" That was it, "Just Do It!" Get up off your ass, take that first step, be the initiator, take control of your life—and that was before the Nike swoosh became an international marketing symbol. That simple advice was as effective as any I'd hear in all the years I went to night school to earn my degree and continue on with graduate studies. Pat Croce, the vocif-erous former president of the Philadelphia 76ers, motivational speaker and entrepreneur, went one step further in his book, *I Feel Great and You Will Too*, in which he exclaims, "Just Do It, Now!"

It took many years before I learned the relationship between achieve-ment and self-esteem. A byproduct of achievement, whether completing a class, earning a degree, getting a promotion, or running a marathon, is confidence. The outcome is no different for someone who learns to play an instrument, masters a craft or writes a short story. And achievement is not possible without taking the first step, but the first step is always the hardest because it takes you out of your comfort zone. There are no magic formulas—Ten Steps, Seven Principles or Five Stages—that begin without a first step. Following up with the second, and third, and so on, is the difference between complacency and achievement. That's it.

Years ago I listened to an interview with James Michener in which he said he didn't consider himself a great writer. He claimed there were many writers much better than himself in the world. According to the Pulitzer Prize-winning author, the difference between himself and a multitude of talented writers who wither in obscurity was that he got off his duff and wrote over forty books, while other writers who possessed as much, if not more talent, talked and dreamed about writing but did nothing.

Frank McCourt, the great Irish author from the lanes of Limerick, and Pulitzer Prize winner himself, instructs his students in *Teacher Man*, "Dreaming, wishing, planning: it's all writing, but the difference between you and the man on the street is that you are looking at it, friends, getting it set in your head, realizing the significance of the insignificant, getting it on paper."

Don't leave your dreams in your head. Act on them. Get them out there—on the track, in the classroom, in the workplace, or on paper, wherever you aspire to do your life's work. Do it for yourself, for your loved ones. Do it for posterity.

· · ·

My training intensity faded as 2004 wound down and I was bored. My list of physical fitness goals for 2005 was blank and I was in a funk. A downturn in my emotional cycle got me wondering if I was going through that stage people my age talk about—that change of life thing. I'd rejected the notion four years earlier when I bought the Harley, but maybe now age was catching up with me. Though I felt lethargic, I avoided entertaining the D word—depressed, at least not in the sense that I was a danger to myself or anyone else. I simply needed ballast in my life to restore equilibrium. My mood was a drastic reversal from the previous several years, a period in which I was generally positive, ambitious and able to conquer any challenge before me. Finally, I realized it was unrealistic to expect to be upbeat every day of my life, so I cut myself a break.

Life was changing drastically and my home, which once resembled a frat house with young people coming and going all hours of the day, was quiet. Jay was married, Col was about to leave to study abroad in Italy, Jimmy moved to Roxborough and Danny bought his first house at the young age of twenty. I watched my world revolve around me as if I were in a dream and all the characters were growing while I got up each morning and followed the same mundane routine. Everyone moved on with their lives, and I hadn't let go and moved on with my own. I was stuck in a dilemma, it was time to practice what I preached—find something I loved, take the first step and Just Do It. I'd read volumes of books, attended too many leadership seminars and taken the Myers-Briggs type indicator test multiple times, and the net result of all the self-evaluation was muddled confusion. I wasn't able to figure out what I wanted to be when I grew up.

I was out for a run on a brisk Sunday afternoon in January while the women were out to lunch before Col departed for Rome. When I finished and walked back to the Jeep in Lormier Park I saw a huge pile of firewood off in the corner of the parking lot. I drove over to the pile just as a Ford Explorer pulled up from the other direction and stopped a few feet away. An older guy jumped out and enthusiastically joined me while we stacked wood into our vehicles—two guys sweating, swearing and talking wood.

That's when a revelation hit me over the head like a two-by-four. It was so obvious that it got lost in the clutter of my everyday routine. Life is about the journey, not the destination. It's not uncommon for people to spend a lifetime searching for their calling, and running was my journey. It was ingrained so deep into the fabric of my being that, without it, I was simply not me. It was as integral a part of my being as breathing, and to ignore it would be like neglecting a key ingredient fundamental to my character. It helped me do everything I did better, more enthusiastically and with more energy. So regardless of what I decided to be when I grew up, if I ever grew up, running had to be part of it.

Introspection

Something seemed to change that afternoon—nothing tangible that I could point my finger at, yet something profound. I took inventory and there were no discernable differences in my life, yet I felt content, a feeling I'd longed for as long as I could remember. It was the same feeling I had when I ran the Delaware Canal on my fiftieth birthday and got a glimpse of the solution—it was the narrative; my message. It was time for me to put into practice those immortal words of Frank McCourt and "get it on paper."

CHAPTER TWENTY-ONE

BOSTON ON MY MIND

Except for knee surgery, I hadn't taken an extended break from running in five years until Mother Nature dumped fifteen inches of snow in January of 2005. A two-week sedentary lifestyle was foreign to me. I was completely disengaged from the activity that was the only constant in my life for thirty-five years. It was an odd feeling, or perhaps a case of divine intervention preventing me from injuring myself again. One afternoon I was lying around reading and came across a marathon training program that wasn't as regimented and time-consuming as others I'd found. Since I would only be able to afford roughly eight weeks of training for the race, allowing adequate time to taper, I decided to adopt it.

In early February I attempted a couple of mid-range runs on consecutive days for the first time in over a month and survived. That weekend I ran a six-miler on Saturday and hooked up with Ed for a thirteen-miler on Sunday. My foot was pain-free from the stress fracture at the end of the run. The following week, daylight was beginning to stretch to six p.m. When I returned from work on Tuesday, I changed into my running gear and headed into Tookany Park and up the trail to Elkins Park Middle School track. When I came down the other side of the hill I recognized Ed's pickup truck off to the side. We hadn't trained together in months and now had run two of the last three days together.

Ed and I had been friends since grade school at Saint Matt's in Northeast Philadelphia. He was one of the few friends I had who possessed intellectual finesse, but was also a frequent tenant in the Vegetable Aisle because he was a wise guy and had trouble behaving. Though we'd taken different roads to adulthood—Ed by way of Villanova University and the Peace Corps, while I was at the University of the Shipyard and volunteer patron at Kennan's Tavern—we always gravitated back together.

Ed was a collegiate boxer; I ran through my apprenticeship. We'd spent years sowing our oats in the pubs of Northeast Philadelphia and rented summer houses at the shore in South Jersey. Equipped with a degree from a prestigious institution, he went on to become a union steamfitter when social work didn't produce the income needed to raise a family with six daughters. It was ironic that we both worked with some of the same welders who would jump between the shipyard and the union. As the years progressed, we were both drawn to distance running and would meet on Saturday mornings for the long run. It bonded us in a different dimension than the trouble we'd instigated as youths.

We had run more road races and trail runs in 2004 than in any other year in our lives. During the second half of the year the training program kicked-in and my times steadily improved. Ed would tell me to run my race, and never held me back. His encouragement played a huge role increasing my confidence. But on this particular Tuesday in mid-February, not quite four months after Steamtown, Ed was pushing me around the track. He was running noticeably stronger and challenging me with each lap. It was a great feeling to watch him run so powerfully as we ran into the dark. I bid Ed farewell on the final lap and ran back down the Parkway trail, squinting to detect any rocks or tree roots so I wouldn't take a nosedive. When I got home I knew my conditioning level was back where I needed it to be, it was the same feeling I had a few weeks before Steamtown.

I was filled with anticipation for a fifteen-miler scheduled for Saturday. More importantly, I was curious how my foot would hold up. It was only two months since the stress fracture and it hadn't bothered me running half-marathon distances—the fifteen-miler would be the test. I went out strong before I settled into a comfortable rhythm. At the turnaround point I was beginning to feel a little tightness where the stress fracture had been, so I proceeded cautiously. I continued at an easy cadence mindful of the injury, but ran effortlessly. When I passed the half-marathon mark the tightness in my foot dissipated and I pressed just enough to fully exert my cardio system, and then turned it up a notch on the three hills leading back to Lormier Park and ran strong to the crest of each hill. I was confident the injury was behind me. I crossed Pine Road with Fox Chase Farm on my left and gazed up at the hills where I'd trained for

Steamtown. I had finished a solid fifteen miles and looked forward to the eighteen-miler scheduled in two weeks.

. . .

Ed coerced me into running the Ugly Mudder, a trail run, the end of February. The Mudder is a seven-mile race in Berks County, PA that requires the endurance equivalent to a half marathon road race because of the mountainous terrain. He didn't have to twist my arm because I attributed qualifying for Boston largely to the endurance training I'd gotten at trail runs the previous year. It was a typical trail run—climbing mountains, scurrying across creeks and jumping over rocks and tree trunks—except for a thirty-foot wall of mud that led to the finish line. Bodies were strewn about the muddy hill, people grabbing legs and limbs of the folks in front of them. Runners caked with muck emerged victoriously at the summit. Inside the clubhouse after the race, frozen runners were warmed with a hot breakfast of pancakes, eggs and bacon, washed down with water, juice and beer. Sugar & Spice, a seventy-something-year-old musical duet, entertained the appreciative crowd of lunatics with authentic Polish-German folk songs, and God knows what else. Such fond moments sealed my fate as a trail runner.

Fully recovered from the Mudder, I embarked on the eighteen-mile run the following Saturday, which went so well I continued past the turnaround point and stretched it into a twenty-miler. Sometimes the aftereffect of a hard workout doesn't hit until a couple days later, and the twenty-miler was one of them—it kicked my ass. I attempted to run Monday thinking I was recovered, but was lethargic and didn't run again until Friday. The four-day layoff felt like an eternity. I ran 10K on Saturday, but my energy level was well below the high of a week earlier.

CHAPTER TWENTY-TWO

ROMAN HOLIDAY

Around the time I was beginning to taper my training for Boston, Joanne and I visited Colleen who was in Rome, ostensibly studying abroad. Col was sharp, always quick to detect when my conversation meandered toward interrogation about the progress of her studies. She'd work me into the corner like a skilled boxer in the ring and hit me with a clever jab, "And how old were you when you graduated from college, Dad?" My arms would drop and I'd be defenseless, because we both knew the answer—forty-three. Oh, she had good moves.

Coincidently, the Rome Marathon was the Sunday we were scheduled to arrive, but with only five weeks remaining before Boston I agreed with Jo that I was out of my mind to even think about entering. In reality, I felt it would be stupid to waste all the training I'd done and blow an opportunity to run the most celebrated race in the world because of needless injury. Colleen ran the 5K race held early the day of the marathon before we got into town, a consolation that made her Pops proud.

On Saturday afternoon, March 12th, Jo and I began our countdown to reunite with Col as we rode to Philadelphia International Airport: two hours until our flight would take off, eight hours to Paris, a two-hour layover, roughly an hour or so flight to Rome and time for the train ride from DiVinci Airport to Termini Station. It would be a fourteen-hour endurance feat with Colleen waiting for us at the finish line. When we arrived at the Air France ticket counter, we were amazed by the large number of people in line to fly to Paris on a Saturday evening, but were more mystified after we went through security and arrived at Gate Seven to board the plane and found it empty. We settled into a couple of seats before I decided to find a currency exchange to trade some US dollars for Euros. When I returned there was a mob at Gate Five across the terminal from where Joanne sat alone. The sign over above Gate Five read Paris—we were off to a good start.

The flight went smoothly with better than average airline food, good wine, an appropriate wine-themed movie, *Sideways*, and a snooze that got us through the night. We were a little frazzled when we got to Paris because the connecting flight number was different from the number printed on our tickets. The language barrier—neither of us spoke a lick of French—complicated the matter, but once we reconciled the two numbering systems, we were eager to plant our butts back into plane seats for Rome. After the layover, only the flight to Rome and train ride to Termini Station remained on our countdown. We finally boarded a plane that appeared slightly advanced from the Wright Brothers' era and sounded even worse, but it got us to Rome, and that was all that mattered.

The landing and baggage claim in Rome were efficient and before we knew it we were on our way to Termini Station on the DiVinci Express. As we entered the city, the train crossed a bridge and I looked down to the street below and saw runners struggling through the final miles of the Rome marathon. Sitting in a comfortable train seat in a foreign country while suffering athletes passed underneath struck me as ironic since I had given a fleeting thought to entering the race myself. I had agonized through debilitating leg cramps at roughly the same stage at Steamtown that these runners were now at in Rome. *That could have been me*, I thought.

The train pulled into Termini Station and we brimmed with anticipation for our reunion with Colleen. Neither our cell phone nor our phone card worked, so I began scouting around for my honey while Jo watched the luggage. After a couple of trips down the platform, I came back and Jo went on a mission to canvass a few potential rendezvous points. No sooner did she leave when a tall, slender young lady with long blond hair turned the corner. We ran toward one another and I swept her off her feet in a huge bear hug and unabashedly kissed her a dozen or so times. When I returned her to earth I told her to run down the stairway in front of us and surprise her Mom. The reunion was consummated and the three of us couldn't stop jabbering as we made our way through town on our way to her apartment.

Rome transformed me from the ranks of the culturally challenged to the marginally enlightened. I was in awe of the overwhelming beauty of the architecture of Old Rome. Colleen was our personal curator, guiding us on walking tours through the narrow, cobblestone streets in neighborhoods that included Trastevere, the Jewish Ghetto and Piazza del Navona and shared with us what she had learned about landmarks such as the Pantheon, Trevi Fountain, Spanish Steps, the Coliseum and innumerable piazzas. We walked, talked, laughed, ate and talked some more, like three kids carrying on in a giant outdoor antique shop.

For a culture that prides itself in its cuisine, food preparation, wine and espresso, I was astonished how difficult it was to find an overweight Roman. I noticed a stark contrast between the Italian attitude toward food and the American philosophy of quantity over quality. Roman cuisine and meal preparation is a timeless celebration of fresh food, herbs and spices, robust flavors, radiant colors and fine wine—it is an art. Conversely, the American super-size, Big Gulp, all-you-can-eat, drive-thru mentality made it easy to spot a fellow countryman from a distance.

Although Old Rome was not conducive to running, with its uneven cobblestone streets, traffic and lunatic motor scooter drivers, I remained relatively fit from a week of constant walking interrupted only by healthy meals of reasonable portions. I was content to live like a Roman, but wondered if the week layoff from the training program would affect the long run I had planned when I returned to the states four short weeks before Boston.

One day we took a train to Venice which was, in Colleen's words, amazing. There is no comparison for an ancient city whose transit system is an amalgamation of waterbuses, water taxis and gondolas. We checked into a Gothic bed and breakfast, dropped off our luggage and hit the town. After a quick lunch we caught a water taxi to the island of Murano where craftsmen had mastered the art of blowing glass into intricate forms since the eleventh century. The incredibly skilled tradesmen hand down their technique from generation to generation, taking twenty years or more to perfect their craft.

When we returned to Venice on the mainland we hired a gondolier, who navigated through narrow canals and pointed out residences along the route where Mozart, Goethe and Marco Polo once lived. It was like a fantasy tour that reminded me of a time when life was simpler and the appreciation of beauty outweighed material possessions. The gondola rocked gently on the water to a therapeutic cadence and I was lulled into a tranquil mood I rarely attained other than on the long run. I watched the gondolier and thought about the stamina and agility it required to propel the heavy wooden craft through the waters of Venice with such little margin of error day in and day out, an endurance feat taken for granted by most tourists. When we arrived back at the dock, I disembarked feeling as though I'd just received a full body massage and didn't want to let it go. For someone who would never be mistaken for a lady's man, I savored the gondola ride with my two sweethearts as the most romantic time of my life.

We returned to the hotel and changed our clothes, and then went out for a night on the town. Our first stop was Piazza San Marco, or Saint Mark's Square, that encompasses Saint Mark's Basilica, Doge's Palace and The Bell Tower. The square is surrounded by endless arches and Gothic detail, and the buildings that line the narrow streets and alleyways around the square are in perfect harmony. We dined on Venetian cuisine, talked, laughed and had the time of our lives; a magical day that I never wanted to end. When we finally returned to the hotel, Jo hopped in the oversize tub for a hot bath and Col and I passed out on the bed—the ideal ending to a perfect day.

We woke Friday morning to a feast of eggs, meats, pastries, yogurt, an assortment of juices and, of course, espresso, in the hotel's historic dining room, with dark oak woodwork that had a warm and homey feel. After breakfast we grabbed our luggage and hurried for the dock to catch a waterbus to the train station for the return trip to Rome. Day-to-day Venetian life fascinated me on the waterbus ride to the San Lucia Station. People loaded on and off at each stop as the vessel snaked its way up the Grand Canal. The mailman, mothers pushing baby carriages, businessmen and women, school children, lovers and people with their dogs transferred at the many stops, as I imagined they had done every day for centuries. Natives carried out their commonplace routine, oblivious to visitors. I was absolutely mesmerized.

A panorama of snow-covered mountains, tiny villages, and miles and miles of vineyards unfurled in the distance outside the train window on the ride back to Rome. The beautiful Italian countryside, interrupted only by short catnaps, made the four and one-half hour ride seem a blur. No sooner were we inside Termini Station, when Col took off to her apartment for a shower, and Jo and I went to the hotel to drop-off our stuff and take a final daylight walk through Old Rome. We meandered through the narrow streets before arriving at what turned out to be our favorite piazza, the Piazza del Popolo, where we enjoyed open-air musicians adjacent to the magnificent obelisk and fountain. At one of the many sidewalk cafés, we sat and enjoyed brochette, pizza and Italian beer. When we were done, we strolled through the narrow streets, in no particular hurry, and shopped for olive oil, wine and a few gifts to take home.

We met Colleen back at the hotel at six o'clock and hopped a bus to her friend Maura's apartment, who went into town with us for our farewell dinner. Maura was also studying in Rome, though at a different school. The two were as dissimilar as two people could be. Maura would flaunt designer clothes and accessories from Neiman Marcus, while Col was more comfortable in casual attire from local shops and boutiques. Maura personified upscale living; Col found glitz hideous and detested drama. A practical person might expect two people with such divergent personalities to repulse one another, but remarkably, despite their differences, they were close friends.

Our final meal was appropriately pasta, brochette, pizza and more Italian beer, an exclamation point to a week-long Italian cuisine lesson that it is impossible to go to a restaurant, or trattoria, in Rome and be disappointed. After dinner, Colleen and Maura took a bus to Termini to meet friends visiting from the States and go out on the town, while Jo and I walked the streets of Trastevere. Sometime in the wee hours of the morning, Col returned to our hotel and curled up in the small bed in the corner of our room to bring a perfect week to an end.

Saturday morning came too quickly. We ate breakfast and called for a taxi to Termini. Colleen insisted on tagging along to say farewell at the train station. Before boarding the Leonardo Express to Di Vinci Airport, we hugged, kissed and hugged some more. It was an emotional time for the three of us after a week together in a romantic ancient city of culture and beauty. The time that transpired between sweeping Colleen off her feet in a bear hug in Termini Station a week earlier seemed like the blink of an eye.

As emotional as it was saying goodbye, I was proud to watch our little girl mature into a vibrant, bright, funny, independent and confident young woman. Leaving her behind on another continent wasn't easy, but I relished a sense of fulfillment on her part. I remembered being filled with trepidation and giving her the fatherly "Men Are Pigs" lecture in January before she departed, her first time in a foreign land with a language she knew very little. Now I left her in Rome, confident in her ability to handle her affairs competently, which made it a bit easier to say goodbye.

. . .

Rome was to the 2005 Boston Marathon what the cruise training program was to the 2001 Philadelphia Marathon, only much closer to race day. I was curious how my body would react when I returned to a different time zone with jet lag after a week layoff from running.

Sunday morning I woke before seven a.m. Eastern Standard Time, one p.m. Rome time. My body was experienced with the three-hour time zone difference of West Coast business travel; however I expected the six-hour time zone difference traveling in the opposite direction to wreak havoc on my biological clock. Sunday afternoon I went for a short four-mile run and other than mild fatigue was pleased with the results. I drew a parallel between our Rome trip and the diversion of the Harley-Davidson and Tae Kwon Do classes I'd taken in 2001 when I was training for my first marathon in twenty years. The lesson from the week-long break was this: it is healthy to temporarily disengage during the course of a long, intense training program—or any long-term grind for that matter.

CHAPTER TWENTY-THREE

MAN PLANS AND GOD LAUGHS

One month remained before I would toe the line in Hopkinton, Massachusetts for the 109th running of the Boston Marathon. I celebrated the occasion with a fourteen-mile run. Considering the week layoff in Rome, I felt surprisingly strong physically and mentally. My confidence intensified as I attacked the final mile, after tackling the hills between Pine and Krewstown Roads in Pennypack Park.

That weekend, I decided to concentrate on the hills during my final long run before the marathon with laps around the Fox Chase Farm trail before crossing Pine Road through Pennypack. I ran a double 5.2-mile out and back, then did two more loops around the farm to cap off a run that contained sixteen hills. I knew I'd be thankful when I approached Heartbreak Hill around mile twenty of Boston. When I finished, I walked back to the Jeep confident that I was ready. I had no calf cramps or foot pain, just that good exhaustion a distance runner savors after a strong twenty-mile run.

Though I didn't train as rigorously as I did for the qualifying marathon, I knew I'd do well. Except for Steamtown, I hadn't been able to break the 3:50:00 barrier since the 1981 Philadelphia Independence Marathon. But my goal wasn't to run a personal record in Boston—it was to savor every second of the experience.

• • •

Running, like life, is a series of highs and lows, and the heights I reached after the twenty-mile run on Saturday was in direct proportion to the depths I'd sink to the following week. I didn't run Sunday and Monday, and resumed with a light-workout Tuesday, planning to conclude the week with some short runs and a moderate ten-miler on the weekend. The weekday runs were sluggish, so I took off a couple more days. The ten-miler became a seven miler. Most times, if I felt sluggish at the beginning of a run and pushed through the first few miles, I was rewarded for my perseverance with increased energy. However, I was in one of those rare funks that disproved my theory. I was outright lethargic.

I began getting soreness in the right knee—my good knee. That was all I needed to convince myself it was time to completely back off. I had just come off a strong fifty-mile week and the last thing I wanted to do was ruin my prospects of running well in Boston at the expense of self-imposed weekly mileage goals. Two weeks before the race I decided it was better to go to Boston after a couple of low-mileage weeks than to go injured.

The first Tuesday of April marked less than two weeks before race day. After some exceptionally miserable March weather, the afternoon began showing promise that spring had arrived. Driving home from work, I got the itch to try out the new Asics I'd bought for Boston. I pulled into the driveway, hurried into the house, changed into my running gear and was out the back door on my way through Tookany in no time. When I got to the track I bumped into Mac, an occasional running buddy, who began asking about the marathon. As often happens when running with a partner, I lost track of time and after Mac finished his run I headed back down the parkway. I had no idea how many miles we had run, but I felt excellent that night. The following afternoon in work I couldn't wait to get back out on the trail and after a second consecutive strong run, my confidence was back. Friday would begin the ten-day countdown.

. . .

Ten days before Boston, my plan took an unexpected detour. On April 8, 2005, I woke up in the middle of the night to empty my bladder, a tendency that had become more common with age; as the saying goes, the older you get the more you pee and the less you sleep. Half-asleep, I made my way down the hallway into the bathroom and stood over the toilet, hitting the bowl by instinct. Alone in the dark and in a stupor, I became lightheaded. I had never fainted in my life, but felt as though I might be going down for the first time. I sat on the toilet seat to finish my business and the only thing I could remember when I regained consciousness was that I had heard the sound of a sickening crunch and saw as many stars as I imagined were in the galaxy. Lying in the darkness, I tried to gather my thoughts to determine whether I was dreaming, but was sidetracked by the cold ceramic tile pressed against my face. When I opened my eyes, I knew something serious had just occurred. After what seemed an eternity, I crawled into the hallway and lay prostrate, slipping in and out of consciousness.

The next thing I remembered was Jo's anxious voice calling from downstairs. Fortunately, she had fallen asleep on the sofa and wasn't with me in bed, or she likely would have found me unconscious on the bathroom floor. I made a feeble attempt to answer as normally as possible so she wouldn't panic. In the most convincing voice I could muster, I assured her that I was fine; just a little woozy. I propped myself onto all-fours, then got to my feet and carefully made my way down the steps, holding onto the railing for dear life. When I turned the corner on the landing and came into her view, I could see the shock on her face. Frightened, she asked what had happened, though she knew from the crash that woke her from a sound sleep that I had taken a terrible fall. I mumbled the little I was able to remember.

Jo guided me into the family room and helped me onto the sofa, and then went into the kitchen to pour some orange juice and make peanut butter crackers. Ironically, it was time for Pope John Paul II's funeral, which we had planned to watch anyway. Since I had such great respect and reverence for him, I wondered whether he woke me in this manner so I wouldn't miss him lying in state. *Some joke, John Paul!* I asked Jo to get me one of the PowerBars I kept in my shoulder bag for emergencies when I traveled on business and didn't have time to eat. Stretched out on the sofa, energy slowly funneled back into my body and I tried to recall what had happened. Suddenly, I became alarmed, What if I can't run Boston? I thought. Or worse yet, What if I could never run again? I wasn't a pessimist and detested drama, but I couldn't stop the stream of possibilities that caused my first fainting spell. Could it have been a coronary episode or blood clot, or something worse?

It was inconceivable for me to imagine life without running. Boston would be only the first disappointment in a future deprived of running. There were alternatives, like cycling and kayaking, but what if I had to completely abstain from endurance sports? My stream of consciousness was heading into a downward spiral and had to be reversed, just as I had admonished the young runner to reject negative thoughts late in the Steamtown Marathon. I concluded that the episode was an anomaly, just a blip on an otherwise healthy screen of life, and I was resolute that nothing would get in the way of running Boston. Nothing!

After the Pope's funeral, I got a shower, dressed and went to work. I had a lot of explaining to do when I walked into the office with a purple eye and swollen face. The story got increasingly sensational, and by quitting time, nobody wanted to mess with me. Joanne learned from a cardiologist in the practice where she worked that a combination of blood loss and urinating could lower blood pressure enough for someone to faint. Then I remembered I had a tooth extracted earlier the previous day and experienced more blood loss than usual. It was a logical explanation I chose to believe. The last thing I needed was for my mind to begin playing tricks and thinking other physiological events were going on inside. For peace of mind I scheduled a physical, but not until after Boston.

When I got home from work that afternoon, the boys, Gina and Jimmy's girlfriend, Alice, came over for a going away meal before they would travel to Rome the following morning to visit Colleen. The boys couldn't keep a straight face when they saw my swollen mug and offered to install handicap bars in the shower and a mechanical chair for the stairway. They were their usual relentless selves, busting my chops about passing out, and they had me laughing uncontrollably about an incident that scared the shit out of me earlier that morning.

Ed called Saturday night, and we made plans for a six-mile run in the morning. The second Ed opened the Jeep door Sunday morning and saw my face, he became hysterical. I told him the story on the way to Pennypack about the episode, and every time he attempted to compose himself, he broke out laughing even harder. What began as an easy six-mile run turned into a relaxing ten miler, and I finished refreshed with no effects from the fainting incident two days earlier. The run was exactly what I needed to restore confidence so I wouldn't be second-guessing that something serious was going on internally.

I restrained from running Monday and tapered the rest of the week. Jo and I did our weekly duty at our parish chapel, and I prayed in thanksgiving for all of my blessings—family, friends, home, job and, after the events of the previous several days, my health. I had the peaceful assurance that I would have divine company on my 26.2-mile journey on Patriots' Day in Boston.

. . .

Tuesday morning I took off to Huntsville, Alabama, to give a presentation at a helicopter industrial base conference. Wednesday would be a work marathon—early wake-up, commute to the Army base, conference, commute to airport, home late—so after I landed and checked into the hotel, I went to find a place to run and came across a municipal baseball complex that had four baseball fields configured to form a huge circle. Luck was on my side; no games or practices were in progress and the gates separating their warning tracks were open, making a large circular track. It was a beautiful, sunny day with a pleasant breeze and not a cloud in the sky—a runner's paradise.

In the middle of the countless laps, I began to think about my long journey to Boston and the thousands of miles I had run in so many places. I thought of all the early morning runs through Tookany Park while Joanne and the kids were still asleep; a trail run in the Rocky Mountains while on business in Colorado that I followed with a ride to visit the massacre site at Columbine High School in the evening; the cruise training program on our twenty-fifth wedding anniversary vacation to Bermuda; so many laps around the National Mall in Washington that I lost count; the Mount Vernon Trail along the Potomac River; running the Seattle, Washington, municipal park trail and climbing Mount Rainier during the week of 9/11; tearing up my meniscus during Captain Bill's ten-mile beach run in Sea Isle City, and limping along a hiking trail in Big Sur the month after I tore the knee to shreds; weight training and baby steps on the treadmill during rehab after surgery; Brian's Run two months after surgery and the Penn Relays Distance Classic 20K three months later; the trail runs that were so instrumental in training for Steamtown; and qualifying for Boston less than one year after my orthopedic surgeon advised me to consider running shorter distances.

The journey to the world's most prestigious road race had been a tapestry of events beginning with the Philadelphia Independence Marathon in 1981, through the 2001 Philly marathon after a twenty-year hiatus, to Steamtown, woven together with the pattern of countless races in between. Fond memories of the places I'd run, people I'd met and things I'd seen reminded me I was doing exactly what I wanted to do, what I needed to do, what I had to do. It defined me. I wouldn't change a thing I'd experienced the previous five years—or fifty years for that matter. Each experience was an ingredient in shaping me, so much so that I was confident the next five years, or fifty, would be better, and I looked forward with optimism and enthusiasm.

The plane didn't land back in Philly until twelve-thirty a.m. Thursday, and I was glad I'd taken advantage of the run in Huntsville. I wasn't concerned, because I hadn't planned to run many miles the week before Boston anyway. I took a five-mile run after work Thursday afternoon and swam with my Special Olympians on Friday night, and then capped off the week with an easy two-mile run on Saturday, strictly to break a sweat and keep the body limber. The remainder of the day flew by cutting and stacking firewood, going to my neighbor's fourth birthday party, and picking up the kids at the airport after their return from Rome in the evening.

. . .

Joanne and I woke Sunday morning to a sunny day; perfect for flying and even better for joining festivities in the city that hosts the oldest and most historic road race in the world. Boston is more than a marathon—it is an epic athletic event that would be run for the 109th time. The Boston Marathon is legend.

There was no way of knowing that Boston was my destination when I led the pack through Pennypack Park during high school football camp decades earlier, and now I was as fit as I'd been during those early days. My passion had been nurtured for more than thirty years and I was mentally prepared, feeling lean, mean and positive. Boston had been in the works all those years and I never knew it until I arrived. It was symbolic of the drive and endurance I'd applied to every aspect of my life—the same determination that catapulted me from the Vegetable Aisle to graduate Cum Laude with a degree in Business Administration, the tenacity that drove me from an apprentice welder to manage an organization full of analysts, the stamina to raise a family and still muster the energy to wake early in the morning and go out late in the evening so I could train for the marathon.

Atypical for a vacation, I ordered a Gatorade in a restaurant at Philly International Airport. Had it not been for the marathon the following day, it would have been a Guinness. I leaned back in a seat and was in a peaceful state of mind, when an announcement came over the intercom that our aircraft was experiencing a mechanical problem. Jo and I looked at one another and I said, "Follow me." I knew from years of business travel that there were flights between the two cities every hour. We jumped up, ran across the terminal and beat the crowd to switch our flight to the next one to Boston. Even with the delay, we arrived before two p.m.

After the plane touched down at Logan International Airport, we hopped on the T, local vernacular for the Massachusetts Bay Transit Authority, for a few short stops to the Courthouse, which was two city blocks from our hotel. It was a beautiful day for walking and we hoofed-it along city streets to the Omni Parker Hotel to drop off our bags before going to the Hynes Convention Center to pick up my race gear and mingle with the crowd at the Expo. Runners and their families and friends had infiltrated Boston and a festive atmosphere throbbed through the city from the Back Bay to the North End to South Boston, or Southie as locals refer to it. Thousands of people packed the Expo, milling through aisles of displays that sold running gear and offered samples of everything from energy bars and spiced rice to Gatorade and iced coffee. Many of the major marathons from around the world including London, Jamaica and New York, had tables set up and were accepting runners' registrations. Every large race has an Expo, but Boston was the largest and busiest I'd ever attended.

The expo spilled into the courtyard outside, with more exhibits and a jazz band playing on stage. We strolled in the warm sun enjoying an assortment of delicious health foods and drinks. The New Balance running shoe company had a creative series of podiums with young athletes posing as sculptures while heckling spectators attempted to make them laugh.

Boylston Street was closed to traffic and runners milled around the brightly painted red, yellow and blue finish line they would cross Monday afternoon, as if it were sacred ground. Jo and I walked out into the street where, in less than twenty-four hours, 18,358 runners, the second largest field in Boston Marathon history, would gut it out through the final city blocks of the race. I was witnessing the marathoner's paradox: a mentality that embraces excruciating pain in order to experience unparalleled exhilaration after crossing the finish line, and then return another day for more. I was one of many runners who solemnly traced the steps we would take the following afternoon in a sort of religious procession, and I caught more than a few glimpses of approval from uncounted strangers. I wasn't alone when I bent down and ran my hand across the smooth, colorful paint. The grandstands on the sidewalk would hold thousands of screaming fans the following afternoon, shouting encouragement to their loved ones at the end of their 26.2-mile odyssey.

Though Jo had been to only a few races with me since my first marathon in 1981, she understood that running was as much a part of me as my legs and feet were. She'd seen me come home late from work or from a long business trip, completely stressed out, then go for an hour run and return revitalized. There were times I would be restless and she'd say, "Why don't you go for a run?" She knew it was my release, no different than her night out with her friends. I was fortunate to have a soul mate who let me be myself, and supported me in whatever wild-ass adventure I embarked on—and I knew it. That she wanted to come to Boston with me was as special to me as her saying, "I do," twenty-nine years earlier.

Sunday evening we went to the pre-race pasta party, an event I avoided at other races, but decided to attend only because it was Boston. I was instantly caught up in the camaraderie, exchanging running stories with those around us while waiting in a line that stretched around the block. I was impressed that thousands of people could be served in an orderly fashion without a food fight breaking out, unlike when my gang would come over our house for a meal. Our table partners were from around the country, including two Catholic priests from Chicago who ran the

Chicago Marathon each year. After dinner we took a walk through Quincy Market before returning to the hotel to get some sleep.

Before drifting off, I read a story about Boston legend Johnny Kelley who finished fifty-eight Boston Marathons, winning in 1935 and 1945. I was humbled by my comparatively modest road to Boston that began as an idea in 2000. Considering how hyped I was after attending the Expo and pasta dinner, I couldn't imagine what was in store for me when I woke on Patriots' Day.

TWENTY-FOUR YEARS TO BOSTON

Patriots' Day in Boston is synonymous with the Boston Marathon, a tradition that locals have worked passionately to celebrate for generations. It is an exhilarating day that combines the world's best marathoners with thousands of amateur athletes and recreational runners into a twenty-six-mile festival. Family, friends, volunteers, and hysterical partiers commingle with fitness disciples who train feverishly for the privilege of pounding their bodies into oblivion. Runners feed off the energy emanating from a frenzied crowd that cheers them the entire course from Hopkinton to Boylston Street.

Unlike most Monday mornings, I welcomed the beeping of the alarm that interrupted my sleep at six a.m. to take a twenty-six-mile bus ride to the small town of Hopkinton, Massachusetts. I snuck out of bed and made my way to the bathroom for my morning constitution and to read the sports page. After I finished the paperwork, I put in my contact lenses, lubed my tender areas and applied sunscreen, dressed, grabbed my bib number, chip, sunglasses and some energy gels. I kissed Joanne lightly on the forehead and tip-toed from the hotel room to her low, peaceful snore. We would reunite ten hours later, after I crossed the finishing line on Boylston Street.

When I stepped outside the hotel door, I was greeted by a perfect marathon day—a tad brisk, not a cloud in the sky or trace of humidity. Directly across the street from the hotel was a line of buses along Tremont Street all the way to Boston Commons where runners were already boarding. I craved caffeine to get through the five-hour wait for the starting gun, so I bought a Café Americano and a *Boston Globe* at Starbucks before the ride to the starting line.

Camaraderie and chatter filled the bus like burners heating air to fill a hot air balloon—a continuation of the atmosphere we'd experienced throughout the entire city from the moment our plane touched down at Logan International Airport. On the ride to the staging area, I talked with an airline pilot from Minnesota who was running his fourth marathon after qualifying for Boston in only his third, and a young woman from New Jersey who was running her first Boston, qualifying in only her second attempt.

My initial annoyance with the long wait for the start of the race disappeared once the bus arrived at Athletes' Village in Hopkinton. The staging area was a conglomeration of entertainers and athletes, food and beverages, and more than a few characters milling around on a grassy field that was perfect for sprawling out to chill. Runners communed, slept, ate, read and relaxed. I lay down with the newspaper and caught up on the sports and news while nibbling PowerBars and fruit and washing them down with Gatorade and coffee. A young woman on the blanket next to me read my favorite book, Steinbeck's *Cannery Row,* which I took as a premonition that it would be a great race. Eventually, I fell asleep. It didn't seem as though five minutes passed when the master of ceremonies made an announcement for the runners to begin walking to their corrals for the start of the marathon.

It was about a mile walk down Grove Street from Athlete's Village to corral number ten, where my pace group assembled for the start of the race. The corrals organize runners by pace group to avoid logjams caused by delusional runners who think they will somehow shave minutes off their mile pace, but instead interfere with faster-paced runners in the early stages of the race. On my way to the corral I talked with a guy who, coincidentally, qualified at Steamtown on his fourth attempt, one time missing, he told me, by only fourteen seconds. I congratulated him on his persistence and wished him well.

About ten minutes after I arrived at my corral, the National Anthem played, and two fighter jets from the Massachusetts National Guard thundered across the sky. Following the National Anthem, Jimmy Durante's *Young at Heart* filled the airwaves in honor of Johnny Kelley who sang the song before the marathon in recent years. Johnny's spirit was among the thousands of runners and hundreds of thousands of spectators, filling the void left by the legend who had passed away the previous October.

The Grand Marshal kept the field of anxious runners up to date on what was occurring at the starting line, roughly a mile from where I stood. The gun sounded and the 2005 Boston Marathon was underway. I squatted, blessed myself and welcomed my Lord along for the ride. The corrals didn't eliminate more than a few false starts as the masses broke into a slow jog only to crash into the runners in front of them, as it would in any race with a field of nearly twenty thousand. The elite runners were well into their second mile before the runners in corral ten ever settled into a sustained jog to the starting line.

Goose bumps rose from my skin in the excitement caused by deafening cheers from the fans that lined West Main Street in Hopkinton. People held signs wishing their loved ones luck in their quest to make it to Boylston Street. Others waved flags from many of the eighty-one countries the runners represented. It seemed there were more spectators on West Main Street than had lined the entire course of other marathons I'd run. By the time I reached the starting line my adrenalin was pumping profusely, and I looked forward to breaking a sweat and settling into a comfortable rhythm.

My priority for the race was to relish every second, knowing that, especially after the fainting spell ten days earlier, tomorrow was never a guarantee. Still, I was tantalized by my preoccupation with time, and found it difficult to ignore that I would re-qualify for the 2006 marathon if I ran at an 8:13 pace. I went out slow on the gentle downhill of the first mile, which was innocent compared to the steep seven-mile drop in the early stages of Steamtown. I caught a glimpse of a sign held by a fan that warned runners, "Go out slow to run fast," and vowed not to repeat the same mistake I'd made when I left Forest City, which likely contributed to the paralyzing calf cramps I suffered in the final miles of my qualifier.

Most marathon fields thin out by the second or third mile of the race and allow ample space for runners to maneuver. Boston was different. Boston never thinned. There was an even flow of runners as far as I could see throughout the entire course.

Music blared in the distance, and I smelled barbeque as the second mile marker approached. I rounded a curve in the road, and ahead on my left was a parking lot full of Harley-Davidsons and a rowdy crowd of bikers partying and screaming encouragement to the runners. The clash of cultures amused me—beer-guzzling bikers cheering athletes who pride themselves on healthy diets, fitness and discipline. The bikers at mile two were boisterous and entertaining and fun. I was tempted to join the revelry, but twenty-four miles still remained.

By mile five I was running a comfortable 8:15 pace, but hadn't settled into the rhythm I'd anticipated. On the rare occasion when I didn't strike a rhythm on a solo run, my mind would drift and devise excuses to cut the run short. The incessant crowd lining the course as it meandered through Ashland, Framingham and Natick took my mind from anything other than enjoying the ride to Boylston Street. From out of nowhere, an Elvis impersonator decked out in the customary white jumpsuit, complete with grommets and stones, pennants swinging freely, and high, thick black hair blowing in the breeze, jogged across from me at curbside for a hundred feet or so. I sucked down my first PowerGel and an energy drink around mile nine and felt the nourishment revitalize my body.

Closing in on the halfway mark, I heard the sound of screaming women in the distance. As I rounded a bend approaching mile twelve, thousands of delirious young ladies had gathered outside Wellesley College. Police barricades held back the mob from attacking the runners, a hint that it wasn't the first time the female student body showed up for the race. They flaunted makeshift signs, many encouraging the runners to stop for a kiss. It was incomprehensible that young college women would have a desire to kiss a sweaty fifty-year-old guy, but I leaned my face into the crowd and patted my cheek as an invitation anyway. There were no takers. The hormones of young guys around me were jumping out of their skin. I said, "I was born thirty years too early, guys," and they laughed. On the way down the hill from Wellesley, I finally found my rhythm.

My adrenalin stabilized after the encounter with my adoring female fans and I anticipated the hills of Newton. The notorious series of hills begins at mile seventeen and culminates at the infamous Heartbreak Hill near mile twenty-one. Before I began my initial ascent, I devoured a second PowerGel hoping for an energy boost, or at least a psychological lift. I repeated a mantra to myself, "Slow and steady," as I began the climb and took advantage of the level grade after each of the three hills for a short recovery. Midway through the Hills, I felt their reputation was earned by their location on the course—roughly three quarters of the way to the finish line—rather than their length and elevation. The hill training on Fox Chase Farm was surely paying dividends as I forged ahead to the ultimate test of a marathoner's resolve—Heartbreak Hill.

A guy many years my senior, wearing a bucket hat, came up from behind on my left. I quietly repeated my mantra to him, "Slow and steady." He turned slightly and gave me a shifty, cockeyed smile as if to say, I'll save you a bagel on Boylston Street, buddy, and continued on his way. I lost sight of him before I reached the top, which I considered a tribute to the senior runners who never quit. The rising tide of yelling and screaming grew louder the farther I progressed to the summit. I saw a face in the crowd that looked like Senator John Kerry, and learned after the race that he often watched the race from the side of the road in Newton. Fans that lined the final stretch to Heartbreak willed the suffering athletes to the crest with fervent and rowdy encouragement. There was no way to measure whether the Heartbreak crowd was the loudest along the course, but there was no doubt they played a huge role in helping the runners tackle the legendary endurance feat.

An enormous inflatable torso draped in a tank top with "Heartbreak Hill" inscribed across its chest was on the front lawn of a house at the summit. My adrenalin pumped so hard that I ran up to some young guys about my kids' age and yelled, "When do the hills begin?" and they responded with a round of chest bumps and high-fives. I was psyched for the conquest into Boston.

The course banked to the left at the top of the hill and rewarded the runners with a long downward slope. I gazed through sweaty eyes at downtown from high upon the hillside. The initial impression was that the remainder of the marathon would be easily achieved, but I knew the final miles would test my spirit and resolve, for I'd just crossed over into the six miles of truth.

Approaching mile marker twenty-two, I saw the time on a digital clock and calculated in my quasi-delirious state of mind that I had no chance to re-qualify, though my goal to savor every moment was shaping into a remarkable success. When I came up on mile twenty-three, a faint tinge of leg cramps sent a message to my brain to proceed cautiously, so I continued at a deliberate pace. The long stretch down Commonwealth Avenue was lined with thousands of screaming spectators. Strangers extended their hands and offered oranges slices, bananas, ice, beer, water, Jell-O shots and several indescribable concoctions to the exhausted runners. Approaching mile twenty-four, my body was completely drained, but the crowd was a reenergizing force.

The venerable Fenway Park appeared on my right, which explained the swelling, boisterous crowd wearing Red Sox hats around mile twenty-five. Running through the center of Red Sox Nation, just blocks from the baseball shrine, I felt appreciation for the persistence of fans that waited decades for a World Series just as I'd waited fifty years to run the world's most celebrated road race. The passion in their voices and enthusiasm on their faces as they shouted encouragement made the cramps in my legs dissipate, if only for a moment.

Shortly after passing mile marker twenty-five, I was hobbled by tightening in my left hamstring. I stopped and dug my fingers into the muscle, kneading it like a mound of pizza dough, and stretched for a few seconds before continuing. *Damn! I ran twenty-five miles and had to stop for a goddamn hamstring of all things, not even a calf.* I started up gingerly, taking shorter strides so I wouldn't aggravate any other leg muscles. I followed thousands of runners in front of me, who were following thousands of runners in front of them, and made a right turn onto Hereford Street for a couple short blocks before arriving at Boylston Street for the final stretch to the finish line.

The twenty-five miles since setting out from Hopkinton nearly four hours earlier was an illusion as I made the final turn onto Boylston Street to finish my work. Tens of thousands of crazies stacked from sidewalk to rooftop greeted the runners. They screamed and partied like it was the middle of Canal Street during Mardi Gras. The agony I encountered moments earlier was extinguished by the delirious fans.

The energy emanating from the crowd on the way to the finish line was contagious. I waved to indistinguishable faces that belonged to spouses, siblings, parents and friends who came to support their loved ones, their eccentric runners, as if they came to see me—and in a sense they did.

After years of watching their runner wake up early in the morning and spend countless hours pounding out the miles, sweating, and enduring—basically living and breathing running—they grew to admire each one of us as a member of the running brother and sisterhood. They grew to understand and appreciate the sacrifice and determination that each runner laid on the street those final city blocks.

I was overcome with emotion. Thirty-five years of running thousands of miles flashed through my mind. I choked back tears of joy. The emotion slowly turned into thanksgiving for the rare opportunity to run 26.2 miles at a stage of my life when most of my friends are happy to finish a round of golf, in a cart. I was grateful to pass in front of an admiring crowd that understood the commitment that each of the 18,358 runners made to be in Boston on Patriots' Day. My body was beat, my legs were cramped, but I never wanted the feeling that warmed my soul to go away. I was down to the last city block, savoring each step and living the moment, knowing only my Lord knew for sure what was in store for me after I crossed the finish line. I looked for Jo, but knew there was little chance of spotting her among the masses. I deliberately took my final steps and jumped lightly on the padded mat at the finish line at 3:54:57, the same finish line where I struck a playful pose for a photo roughly twenty-four hours earlier, and the same finish line that John Kelley crossed fifty-eight times on Patriots' Days' past.

The culmination of work, determination and pain seemed to force every emotion I had experienced in fifty years to erupt. My eyes were blurred from tears. My vision was too clouded to see what was going on around me. Though I was humbled by the crowd who applauded the achievement of the runners, I knew in my heart there were many more courageous people in the world worthier of applause than me. I thought of Dick Hoyt who pushed his son Rick, born with cerebral palsy, in a wheelchair the entire race every year since 1981, and the courage of the tall blonde with the deformed arms who passed me on Kelly Drive during two Philly Marathons. I was reminded of all of the people with medical challenges who woke each morning and expended the energy equivalent to running a marathon just to get out of bed and make it through the day. I thought of my selfless sister, Jeannie, who pleasantly navigates life with multiple sclerosis, always smiling and insisting on doing for others while never asking for anything. They were the courageous ones who had no crowd applauding their daily achievements and never got a medal when they successfully conclude another day. Then I smiled at the promise and hope of living in a world filled with such heroes.

Slowing to a deliberate walk, I gazed around for my honey as I made my way through a mass of volunteers serving water, fruit and energy bars to replenish the multitude of depleted bodies. I stripped the shirt from my back and felt the warm afternoon sun against my chest while I walked gingerly to the curb and bent down to untie my lace and remove the chip. When I got up, a pleasant elderly woman approached and wrapped the foil around me that keeps a runner's body heat from escaping. As I walked from the restricted runners' area, a young woman came up, put a medal around my neck and congratulated me. It was the first of many congratulations I received before I left Boston.

Triumphant in my pulverized body, I limped along Berkeley Street and turned right on St. James to the family meeting area. I peered through streams of dried salty sweat which had diffused across the surface of my sunglasses as if I were looking through a kaleidoscope. I scanned the temporary signs affixed high on the street lamppost with the letters of the alphabet. The letter "B" where Joanne and I agreed to rendezvous after the race was up ahead. I tried to stand on the tips of my toes to see over the mass of humanity, but my five-foot, nine-inch frame felt as though it had been beat down to about five-foot, one from the pounding it had taken.

Suddenly, I saw a familiar face about ten feet from a lamppost on the sidewalk between the curb and a building. I waved both arms above my head and yelled. She turned and her unmistakably striking blue eyes met mine, eyes with the same glimmer that hooked me twenty-seven years earlier. *It was those eyes, always those eyes.* We nudged our way through the crowd toward one another and embraced, like two lovebirds that hadn't seen one another in half a lifetime. Just as I was about to sweep her off her feet, my calves tightened like steel cables supporting the weight of a suspension bridge and I steadied myself by holding onto her shoulders to keep from falling.

Jo sat me carefully against the building and kneaded my aching calf muscles. A measure of relief returned to my face and she smiled, reached into a bag, pulled out a new warm-up jacket and draped it over my shoulders and said, "Congratulations." She knew I'd never buy a memento for myself, but took a hunch I wouldn't object to wearing a jacket bearing the logo of the Boston Athletic Association.

The prospect of sleeping on the street as a vagrant increased with each passing minute my aching, sweaty body pressed against the cold concrete, so Jo helped me to my feet. I braced against the building for balance before we limped through town. As we crossed the Boston Commons back toward the hotel, complete strangers offered congratulations as though I were a celebrity. Accepting congratulatory gestures is one of the roles a runner fulfills in Boston on Patriots' Day. It didn't matter that I crossed the finish line in 8,647th place, I was as happy as Hailu Negussie who came in first at 2:11:45 to win the $100,000 purse.

We stopped and sat on a bench at the side of the pond and watched swans paddle and children play at the water's edge. I'd always loved that special runner's soreness, but never as much as the one I had sitting on the park bench in the Commons. There aren't many occasions when a smelly, disheveled lout clad in dried, salty perspiration could get away with sitting arm-in-arm on an inner-city park bench with an attractive, stylishly dressed woman without drawing curious looks—this was one of those rare occasions. After a while we looked at each other and nodded; a signal to make the final push to the Omni Parker.

Jo stood up and helped me to my feet. Once I took the first few steps I was able to manage a forward-progressing limp at a pace much different from the rhythm I'd enjoyed earlier in the afternoon. As we made our way down Tremont Street to the hotel, my mind drifted to a hot tub and sink full of ice-cold pale ale. It was hard to determine if I was in heaven or in Boston, or perhaps Boston is heaven to a marathoner on Patriots' Day.

Jim and daughter Colleen after qualifying for the Boston Marathon at the Steamtown Marathon in Scranton, Pennsylvania in October 2004.

The Brennan clan has multiplied since the 1981 Philadelphia Marathon. From bottom left: Gina, Colleen, Alice, Monty, Jim, Jason Jr, Carley, Joanne, Dan, Jason, Jim Jr.

EPILOGUE

The finish line on Boylston Street was the beginning of new and exciting adventures. In January of 2006, I won my first running award ever, a bronze medal for placing third in my age group at the Bermuda International Marathon. I was presented the award by the Premier of Bermuda at the packed Harbor View Ballroom in the Fairmont Hamilton Princess Hotel.

Four months later my email address on the registration list for the Broad Street Run caught the attention of a reporter for the *Philadelphia Daily News*. He wrote to me and requested an interview, figuring anyone with runjimrun buried in their email address must have a few stories to tell. I didn't disappoint him. We talked for about half an hour and then I went to the newspaper building on North Broad Street for a photo session with a young photographer.

The day the article was scheduled to go to press I bought the newspaper on my way to work. I furiously paged through the paper in the store parking lot looking for my mug and missed it the first time through, so started over a bit more deliberately. As I ascended the page numbers passing through the news, editorials, food and, finally, the end of the sports section, I found the tiny paragraph on page seventy-two, next to the Pep Boys tire ads. I was a legend, if only in my own mind.

In June I was at a leadership seminar in Denver and registered for the Run the Rockies Half-Marathon in Frisco, Colorado. Frisco is situated in Summit County at an elevation of over nine thousand feet above sea level. I was an East Coast native accustomed to running nine thousand feet closer to sea level, but spent three weeks in Denver training after class each day and was as prepared as I could possibly be.

I adjusted to the altitude the first few miles after we left the starting line at Copper Mountain and ran a surprisingly strong race. At a turnaround point in the final miles I noticed there were not many runners my age competing, so I turned up the tempo a bit. After I sprinted through the finish line, I walked into a pavilion and approached a woman on the race committee to find out where I had placed, but the results were not yet in. I had an early afternoon flight back to Philly, so I went to my hotel, showered and packed. I stopped back at the pavilion on my way out of town and learned that I placed third in my age group once again, my second running award of 2006. With little time to spare, I downed a celebratory beer and then broke the Colorado state speed limit all the way to Denver International Airport.

After a lifetime as a distance runner and marathoner, 1 lost the desire to achieve time goals. Once I was no longer driven to qualify for a race or place for an award, running became more enjoyable. I no longer trained feverishly for races the way I did for the Boston Marathon, instead I simply maintained a level physical conditioning I'd reached somewhere in the midst of the most intense training program I'd ever followed.

I am always mindful of how fortunate I had been to run long distances for so many years, but never so much as in 2009 when I underwent two knee surgeries and my orthopedic surgeon told me on both occasions that I had, "more arthritis than I'd like to see in a guy your age." He recommended that I consider running shorter distances, like the 5K or 10K—and definitely not more than a half-marathon. It was hard advice to swallow, but at fifty-five I had to begin thinking long-term. The question became, did I want to moderate so I could be active into my seventies or, hopefully, even my eighties, or continue to pound my knees into oblivion and end my running days before I reached sixty? I resigned to the notion that my marathon days were over.

My adjusted fitness routine included running shorter distances combined with more cycling, weight training and low-impact aerobic exercises, but I missed the euphoric feeling of a soaking perspiration and clarity of mind that came only while on a long run. I began running almost exclusively on soft surfaces and entered more trail runs. Trail running became a blessing and revived my otherwise directionless running life.

After two years of following this modest exercise routine, something unexpected happened—I began to push beyond 10K distance again. I had no intention to extend beyond the 10K, but inadvertently discovered that my knees no longer ached after a six-mile run, so I kept going. I completed a 20K and a half-marathon in 2011 and ran my first marathon in four years in November 2012. I now see no end in sight to the possibilities, including my first triathlon in 2013.

. . .

With age comes perspective. I realize that the journey to Boston was never really about Boston, just as the Philly Marathon in 1981 was never really about Philly. It took every one of those years and each mile along the way before I realized that running was its own reward. The solace and contentment I'd found within the long run maintained balance in every aspect of my life. Distance running enabled me to get beyond an underachieving childhood, persevere through years of night school to earn a degree, raise a family and manage a hectic, though successful career. When I look back at these achievements I see them woven into my quest to run the Boston Marathon.

Solitude on the trail gave me time to look within and uncover meaning in all my effort. An hour run enables me to dig into the essence of my existence and I realize I am simply a flawed human being navigating through the complex maze of life. Running added stability, richness and purpose that drove me to achievements I never would have dreamed, and today running is my partner as a writer. When my brain stops working and the computer screen is blank, I lace em up and hit the trail. Many articles and short stories I've published were inscribed in the gray matter of my mind while I was running through the forest or in the meadow with only my thoughts and occasional livestock to keep me company.

In a sense, I found the marathon a metaphor for life. Had I not set out to conquer the 26.2-mile challenge in 1981, I am quite certain my story never would have found its way onto these pages.

Index